THE DICTATORS

"Good introductory material . . . will stimulate teenage interest."

—*School Library Journal*

"As a crash course in fundamentals, it has its distinct virtues, and it gives a net impression of the absolute hell this century has been through. The author has a wonderfully simple point of view: dictators who died poor are better than dictators who died rich."

—*The New York Times Book Review*

THE DICTATORS

WHO THEY ARE AND HOW THEY HAVE HAVE INFLUENCED OUR WORLD

THE DICTATORS

WHO THEY WERE AND HOW THEY INFLUENCED OUR WORLD

JULES ARCHER

Foreword and Update by Brianna DuMont

Sky Pony Press

NEW YORK

Historical texts often reflect the time period in which they were written, and new information is constantly being discovered. This book was originally published in 1967, and much has changed since then. While every effort has been made to bring this book up to date, it is important to consult multiple sources when doing research.

Visit our website at www.skyponypress.com.

10 9 8 7 6 5 4 3 2 1

Library of Congress Cataloging-in-Publication Data is available on file.

Series design by Brian Peterson
Cover photo credit Associated Press

Print ISBN: 978-1-63450-163-7
Ebook ISBN: 978-1-63450-896-4

Printed in the United States of America

To Dane Archer in the hope that his knowledge of psychology and anthropology, from his studies as an exchange student in post-Hitler Germany and now in his final year at Yale, will support his father's findings about dictatorship.

CONTENTS

FOREWORD   xi

TIMETABLE: THE RISE AND FALL OF A DICTATOR   xv

1   THE NATURE OF A DICTATOR   1

2   SOVIET UNION   11
    I.   Lenin   12
    II.   Stalin   21
    III.   Khrushchev   29

3   ITALY   38
    Mussolini   38

4   TURKEY   47
    Atatürk   47

5   CHINA   55
    I.   Chiang Kai-shek   56
    II.   Mao Tse-tung   63

6   CARIBBEAN DOMINICAN REPUBLIC   72
    Trujillo   73

7   CUBA   81
    I.   Batista   81
    II.   Castro   86
    HAITI: Duvalier   98

8   PORTUGAL   105
    Salazar   105

9 GERMANY   114
     Hitler   114

10 SPAIN   124
     Franco   124

11 INDONESIA   134
     Sukarno   134

12 YUGOSLAVIA   144
     Tito   144

13 ARGENTINA   154
     Perón   154

14 EGYPT   162
     Nasser   162

15 DICTATORSHIP VERSUS DEMOCRACY   173

AFTERWORD   182

BIBLIOGRAPHY   185

INDEX   189

FOREWORD

The word "dictator" conjures up images of angry little men with bad facial hair, but the Adolf Hitler-type isn't the only definition. In fact, defining dictators is where it gets tricky.

In his first chapter, Archer does so with a story—a fictionalized tyrant's rise and fall. Taken from the real lives of his eighteen dictators, the mashup could read like a blueprint: How to Live (and Die) Like a Dictator.

Step One: Be born a peasant.

Step Two: Tell the masses you're saving them from something worse (their predecessor, a horrible future, other power-hungry nations, etc.).

Step Three: Get a cool nickname. Generalissimo, Il Duce, or Big Boy all work.

Step Four: Organize your muscle to better terrorize the masses once they've bought what you're selling. You'll also need a tight inner circle of lackeys to do your bidding.

Step Five: When in doubt, start a war. If people are focused on an outside enemy, they won't see that your domestically-challenged dictatorship really isn't putting food on the table.

This should buy you at least a few years, maybe even decades-worth of power in order for you to secretly squirrel away a fortune to buy a private island where you will flee (if you're lucky) after your inevitable fall. Sorry.

These guidelines may make it seem like all dictators are created equal, but they aren't. Not all dictators are terrible people, bent on world domination. While dictators of the Right align themselves with the military and the ruling classes, often to prevent social unrest and revolution, dictators of the Left align themselves with the struggle of the oppressed classes. Sick of the awful standard of living in their countries, these dictators rise to power on grandiose ideas of the redistribution of wealth and creating a better world for all.

Regardless of their leanings, the lives Archer recounts here are hard to read at times. Collectively, these dictators oppressed and killed hundreds of millions of people to keep their power, and their brutality, like that of Mao or Stalin, was legendary. In hard times, people support crazy when nothing else is working.

Adolf Hitler is the classic example. Germany was full of intelligent, hardworking men and women, and getting a German education was an ivy-covered privilege. After WWI, however, war reparations and hard times forced the German people to look elsewhere for their bread and Wiener Schnitzels. Hitler promised a return to glory days. From there, it was one tiny step after another to crazy dictator for life.

Dictators thrust themselves into power by promising good times for all. Some even succeeded—to an extent. Fidel Castro was tall, dark, and handsome. Even Archer sort of liked him, calling Castro a "genuine hero uncorrupted by greed for riches or triumph." Castro did overthrow the previous dictator, Fulgencio Batista, and he did make life better for many Cubans. But that doesn't mean Castro wouldn't also throw you in front of a firing squad for his ideals.

Archer sees the ambiguity of such figures and presents both sides. But he clearly appreciates some dictators more than others. Take Josip Broz Tito of Yugoslavia for example. Archer holds him up as a standard bearer for the "enlightened" or "benevolent" dictator. Only problem, Tito wasn't dead yet. He died in 1980, a little over a decade after Archer wrote about him.

That's the danger in writing about still-living dictators. Their legacies aren't set. By today's standards, Tito's legacy is mixed, at best. In 2011, Slovenian courts ruled that streets named after Tito were unconstitutional because it had been found that Tito had severely limited human rights in his quest to unite the Balkans. That's not to mention the fact that after his death, the Balkans fell to horrible wars for over a decade. The backlash against Archer's "war hero" had begun.

While Archer plays some favorites, he doesn't hide from the dictators' bad sides. He freely admits that even with good intentions, their methods could be brutal. In some of these dictators' countries, it wasn't until the 21st century that people were able to step back and recognize the suffering amidst the saving. And feelings are still mixed, because it's complicated and complex to love or hate a person who both modernized their countries and suppressed millions. In Turkey, Atatürk stepped out of the ruins of the Ottoman Empire and took his people with him into the modern world. Of course, he also took out anyone who didn't like his methods or his madness. See? Complex.

For the sake of completeness and readability, I've seamlessly updated the fates of every dictator still alive when this book was first published in 1967 into Archer's original text. To give you some idea of the times Archer was writing in, I'll tell you that the only corpses were Vladimir Lenin, Josip Stalin, Benito Mussolini, Mustafa Kemal Atatürk, and Adolf Hitler.

Perhaps even crazier than that, in the 70s and 80s, Third World countries had a rotating door of uprising and revolutions. One came in while another went out. The dictator roll call read like a who's who of genocide. Archer didn't get to talk about Pol Pot's Cambodian genocide, the "Butcher of Uganda" Idi Amin, or Libya's eccentric Muammar Gaddafi, because all those atrocities were in his future.

THE DICTATORS

We'd like to think our world is radically different from half a century ago—dictators are of his present, not ours. Unfortunately, that isn't true. As long as there is poverty and inequality, there will be dictators. And if Archer teaches us anything in this book, he teaches us how easily one comes to power under the guise of a savior.

TIMETABLE: THE RISE AND FALL OF A DICTATOR

August 29, 1934. Josip Fralini is born in a mud hut in Bulvakia. His parents are half-breed peasants in a country where the people are wretchedly poor. Bulvakia is ruled by a corrupt Parliament of aristocrats under King Alfredo IV.

January 14, 1950. Extremely bright, Josip wins a scholarship to study for the priesthood in the Bulvakian Orthodox Church. Reading Marxist books in secret, however, turns him against the church. At nineteen he leaves the monastery to take a law clerk's job at beggarly pay.

August 7, 1958. He becomes the student and disciple of Alexander Lenovar, a great liberal lawyer and crusader for social reform. The corrupt royalist regime tolerates Lenovar's criticism as simply token opposition.

May 1, 1962. May Day. Encouraged by Lenovar, Fralini leads a demonstration against the government. The King's troops attack the crowd. One hundred twelve persons are killed. Fralini is arrested and flung into jail.

June 4. A small group of admirers bribes a guard and helps Fralini escape to Karteg, center of the peasant protest movement. He organizes his followers into an armed band.

July 10. With their ranks swelled by recruits, Fralini leads them in raids on large feudal estates. They seize arms, kill aristocrats, and dynamite some mansions.

July 21. Bulvakian Army forces, led by General Misha La Grande, surround Karteg at midnight. Trapped, Fralini and his aides are arrested and jailed again.

September 16. Accused of leading the dynamite raids of July, Fralini cries to a crowded courtroom, "I not only admit it—I am *proud* of it! My followers and I will never stop fighting until Bulvakia is free of tyranny!"

September 19. He is exiled from Bulvakia. He escapes the death sentence only because the government fears making a martyr of him and inflaming popular discontent.

October 30. Alexander Lenovar feels the time is ripe for a liberal opposition movement. He begins to build the Bulvakian People's Party in secret.

March 4, 1963. Disguised by a beard, Fralini steals back into Bulvakia with a forged passport and a new name—Casmir. He joins Lenovar, who needs funds for the Party.

April 11. Casmir leaves for the south of Bulvakia with a small band of "men of action" like himself, to begin a series of daring bank and mail-train robberies.

October 2. With plenty of money on hand, Casmir begins building a strong Party organization in southern Bulvakia.

November 10. On signal from Lenovar, he leads a peasant uprising against some big plantations. The landowners are driven out of the province.

January 19, 1964. Casmir divides up the land among the peasants and sets up village cooperatives.

February 3. Fearing full-scale revolution, the King's ministers advise an old trick—uniting the country behind the government by warning of a threat of invasion from tiny Pogary to the west. Propaganda broadcasts begin.

March 8. Bulvakian forces are mobilized for war.

March 19. In the Party's paper, *The People's Voice,* Lenovar denounces the government for trying to drag the Bulvakian people into an imperialist war of aggression.

May 21. Lenovar and Casmir clash violently over tactics. Casmir wants to call for a week of uprisings to stop war preparations. Lenovar refuses, afraid this would give Parliament a pretext for using the Army to crush the Bulvakian People's Party and censor *The People's Voice*. Reports seep out that the two men are not speaking to each other.

August 7. Casmir is expelled from the Party.

November 16. A new paper appears, *The Bulvakian Masses*. It calls upon the nation's workers to support a war on Pogary, pointing out that revolution thrives in wartime. Publisher and editor of the new paper is Casmir.

November 25. Lenovar denounces him as a traitor to the working-class movement, and accuses him of having made a deal with the government. Where, otherwise, did Casmir suddenly get the money to publish an expensive new paper?

January 1, 1965. Casmir leads a mass pro-war demonstration to the steps of Parliament.

January 2. The Bulvakian Parliament votes unanimously to declare war on Pogary. The King signs a proclamation.

May 12. Casmir volunteers for the infantry.

July 18. Wounded, saving two soldiers under fire, he is decorated for bravery. Accepts promotion to corporal, but refuses officer's commission. "I came from the common people," his paper quotes him as saying, "and I shall always stay one of them—in war and in peace!"

October 3. Pogary sues for peace.

December 8. Casmir returns to edit his paper.

February 12,1966. Bulvakian People's Party directs a nationwide demonstration against the government. There is postwar chaos—no jobs, a scarcity of food, inflation, a housing shortage. New thousands join the Party.

March 2. A delegation of aristocrats, rich manufacturers, and land barons calls on Casmir in secret. They offer to pay for and equip a private army of veterans, with Casmir as their general, if he will crush the Bulvakian People's Party. His reward: a seat in Parliament.

June 20. Lenovar directs an uprising against the King.

June 21. Huge crowds take over public buildings in the name of the new Republic of Bulvakia. The Army is torn by indecision. Some troops go over to the people, some fight them. Civil war rages for almost a week.

June 28. Casmir double-crosses his backers by offering Lenovar the support of eight thousand troops he controls, in exchange for appointment as second in Party command. Lenovar agrees.

June 30. The revolution triumphs. The King flees abroad.

July 1. Parliament dissolves. Lenovar fills its empty seats with members of the Party.

July 2. Huge victory celebrations all over Bulvakia.

July 26. In a lightning move, Casmir suddenly ousts Lenovar from leadership of the Republic, placing him under arrest for treason. The charge against Lenovar is "fostering a cult of personality"—seeking personal power.

July 28. After a carefully arranged demonstration on his behalf, Casmir appears in Parliament. Stooges hail him as "Casmir the Incorruptible." He promises the new Republic shall become "a great paradise for Bulvakian workers, peasants, and patriots." Members are compelled to rise and swear an oath to defend the life of their new leader.

August 13. In a surprise move, Lenovar's supporters in Parliament propose and win a vote for national elections.

August 14. Casmir dissolves Parliament as "a nest of traitors," and has all the doors bolted shut.

August 20. Lenovar is given a secret trial and sent into exile. There is a tacit understanding among Bulvakian revolutionary leaders that the penalty for losing a struggle for power should be exile, rather than execution.

September 1. The nation's controlled press begins a chorus of praise for "Casmirism"—the new movement which is going to "rebuild Bulvakian society."

September 10. Casmir ousts General La Grande, taking over control of the Army as Generalissimo. Some high officers opposed to him are exiled. Those he needs are bribed with opportunities for graft and plunder. To purchase the loyalty of the troops, he raises the Army's pay.

October 1. His first Five-Year Plan begins. To change Bulvakia from an agrarian to an industrial nation, he asks the people to work long hours for low pay. Their patriotic sacrifice will build the factories and heavy machinery the nation needs. Casmir promises they will be rewarded by a better life in just a few years.

October 10. He puts every corporation, labor union, and municipal and social organization under his control. Companies to which he awards government contracts pay him "executive dividends," deposited for him in bank accounts overseas.

November 3. Begins nationwide program of building roads, dredging harbors, digging irrigation ditches. Issues strict orders that all trains must run exactly on time. New public buildings, stadiums, and statues are built in the capital. When the State Treasurer complains that the government has no money left, Casmir snaps, "Print more!"

November 21. New posters everywhere educate the people in "the new culture of Casmirism." They must wear shoes in public. All streets must be kept clean. Fingernails must not be dirty. "Bulvakians—be worthy of the Generalissimo!"

December 3. General La Grande leads a desperate counter-revolution with a small force. He is swiftly defeated.

December 7. La Grande is reported a "suicide" in jail.

January 15, 1967. "Night of the Long Knives." Forty Party officials are murdered in their beds after midnight, as Casmir purges all he suspects of unreliable loyalty, or as dangerous rivals for power.

March 6. He forms the Casmirist Youth Corps. Black-uniformed youths of ten to sixteen are to be given knives, taught Party slogans, used to break strikes. Medals will reward those who report parents for "unpatriotic" remarks. Corps motto: "Believe, Obey, Fight—for the Generalissimo!"

May 7. First elections of the Republic. Voters have a choice of voting for or against Casmir as President. There are no other candidates. He wins a "sweeping victory."

June 10. Denied loans from abroad, Bulvakia's shaky economy begins to collapse. Banks and businesses shut down; workers are thrown out of jobs; food piles up unmarketed and unsold. Spontaneous riots break out in the cities.

June 20. Casmir broadcasts a thundering accusation against "the real cause of Bulvakia's troubles—the traitorous Jens of the world, who hate us and want to see us starve to death!" He orders a pogrom against Bulvakia's Jens.

June 21. Jens are stoned, tortured, and burned alive.

June 30. Casmir gives the people another scapegoat—the Lenovariks. "Any worker who talks against the government, or against the President-Generalissimo—*he* is a Lenovarik traitor!" Secret police make thousands of arrests.

August 1. Casmir wins a fifteen-million-dollar loan from the great Federal States by convincing them Bulvakia is in danger of being overthrown by Chipanese revolutionaries operating in Bulvakia. There are exactly seven Chipanese in all Bulvakia, but the Federal States doesn't know that.

August 8. By instigating worker riots, Casmir takes over and nationalizes eighty million dollars' worth of foreign-owned factories. He sells some secretly to Bulvakian tycoons.

September 20. Treasury full once more, Casmir orders government stores to sell black bread and rice wine at low prices to peasants and workers to allay unrest.

September 27. Nations whose investments have been confiscated stop trading with Bulvakia.

October 18. To convince the people all is well, Casmir puts on great public spectacles. Huge crowds flock to see these shows and circuses. Often the pressure of the crowd is so great that people are crushed to death.

December 23. Casmir elevates Bulvakian Orthodox Church to position of a state religion; all other religions are forbidden. The High Patriarch calls Casmir "a great patriot and a devout servant of the Lord."

December 27. Treasurer warns economic boycott is bankrupting Bulvakia. Factories shutting down; unemployment spreading; farmers with unsold crops forming angry mobs.

January 31, 1968. Civil war breaks out in neighboring Gerfrancia.

February 8. Casmir declares war on northern Gerfrancia, hoping war will avert a domestic crisis, and a wartime economy will provide jobs. He also hopes for victor's spoils.

February 10. High Patriarch blesses his "holy crusade."

February 21. Lenovar returns secretly from exile.

March 26. Draftees revolt against being sent to intervene in Gerfrancia's civil war. Some officers shot.

April 5. Anti-war demonstrations break out all over Bulvakia, led by supporters of Lenovar.

April 12. Troops and workers join in a mass attack on government buildings. Their revolution succeeds.

May 4. Casmir flees the country in disguise.

May 8. He arrives in Pogary, which has offered him asylum. He will live here in exile on the fortune banked for him while he was Generalissimo of Bulvakia, The fortune is estimated at between eight and fifteen million dollars.

If the story of the rise and fall of the dictator Casmir has a strangely familiar ring, there is a reason.

It is made up of actual events which took place in the lives of eighteen different dictators. Only names of people and places, and a few minor details, have been changed.

Casmir is the prototype of all the dictators, past and present, profiled in this book. Despite their individual differences, they share many basic similarities in the way they come to power, hold power, and topple from power.

Their lives are important to us because they have, to a large extent, shaped much of the world we live in, and will continue to do so for generations to come. Since we will have to share the earth with them during our lifetime, we had better understand as much about them as we can.

The peace of the world depends upon it.

I

The Nature of a Dictator

What *is* a dictator? In simplest terms, he is a ruler who seeks and gets absolute powers of government, usually without regard to the expressed wishes of the people. He may come to power legally, then hold on to it by force; or he may seize power illegally. He differs from an absolute monarch basically in that he has no hereditary claim to rule, no recognition on that score by the nobility or the people, and no traditions of responsibility to his subjects.

Why is he permitted to get so much power? Often the people have no choice, if he takes command at the head of an army. Sometimes they are ignorant of his intentions, or indifferent to national politics. In many cases their lives are so miserable that they are willing to surrender their liberties to a "strong man" in the desperate hope that he has easy solutions to their difficult problems.

New and faster communications in the twentieth century have inadvertently produced a rise in dictatorships. In a shrinking world, people of "have-not" nations have become aware of the high standard of living enjoyed by people in the "have" nations. This has led to growing frustration and unrest. In some underdeveloped countries, local revolutionists have fought for and won dictatorial powers to industrialize the backward economies of their nations by regimentation. These are the dictators of the Left, dedicated to a classless society in which all share the wealth equally.

In other underdeveloped countries, frightened ruling classes have sought to prevent revolution and loss of their power by using dictators to control popular unrest through fear, terror, and deception. These are dictators of the Right, dedicated to regimentation on behalf of a class society.

As long ago as 1830, Alexis de Tocqueville, the celebrated French jurist, predicted that one day the world would be divided into two camps—one in which people were ruled by tyranny, the other in which they were governed by their consent. By the mid-1960s, more than half the people on earth did not live under a democracy as we understand it.

Of the world's 3.2 billion people at the time, about forty per cent were in democracies similar to the United States. Another forty per cent lived under totalitarian rule; and twenty per cent belonged to countries that were mixtures of democracy and dictatorship.

The word "dictator" comes from the Latin *dictare:* to say. This term for "the man who has the say" was used for the first time in 501 B.C, when the two consuls who jointly governed the Roman Republic found it necessary to be absent from Rome at the same time to lead armies in the field. They appointed a deputy to govern with sole power in their name: a dictator.

Later, a dictator was also appointed in times of great emergency, as when Rome was faced with civil war. As a warning to the people, the dictator would be preceded through the streets by *aediles,* or magistrates, bearing ceremonial axes as symbols of his power. In time of war, he would lead the armies and decide all civil matters pertaining to the war.

"When there were two consuls sharing power equally," the Roman historian Livy tells us, "it had been possible to appeal from one to the other; but from a dictator there was no appeal, and no help anywhere but in implicit obedience." With a dictator, too, no valuable time would be lost during national emergencies because of two consuls squabbling over decisions.

he had 117 suspects shot without trial. Thousands of old Bolsheviks were accused as traitors in secret trials, then shot. Trotsky was charged with plotting in exile with Germany and Japan to attack the Stalin regime. The press abroad scoffed, branding the plot a propaganda hoax.

Stalin angrily ordered public trials with foreign correspondents present. Many of the defendants, faced with incriminating evidence, confessed. Among them were Kamenev and Zinoviev, who implicated Trotsky. "The proceedings established clearly the existence of a political plot and conspiracy to overthrow the government," reported Josip E. Davis, then U.S. Ambassador to Russia.

The purges went on for four terrible years. Yagoda, the secret service chief who sent the first thousands of accused men before the firing squad, was then arrested himself and executed. The same fate overtook his successor, Yezhov. Old Bolsheviks whispered that Stalin wanted their lips sealed.

It was not until March 1939, that Stalin finally told a Party Congress, "Undoubtedly we shall have no further need of resorting to the method of mass purges." By that time, he had frightened every Bolshevik official into subservience.

With the Red Army seriously weakened by the purges, Stalin kept a worried eye on Nazi Germany and Fascist Italy. He suspected that these avowed foes of Communism were being secretly encouraged to attack the USSR by England, France, and America. They had made no attempt to stop Hitler from capturing republican Spain for Franco, or from swallowing up Czechoslovakia. The Nazi arrow pointed east at Moscow.

Stalin urged the democracies to join him in a mutual aid pact. When London and Paris rebuffed him coldly, he warned them grimly, "The Russians will not allow themselves to be used as cannon fodder for the capitalist powers!"

He threw a bombshell into the Western camp by suddenly signing a "nonaggression pact" with Hitler, the two agreeing to divide Poland between themselves. Liberals all over the world were shocked and disgusted by Stalin's willingness to cooperate with Nazi Germany. But for the Kremlin boss, a true dictator, the ends once again justified the means.

By taking eastern Poland, he kept Nazi divisions off Soviet borders. If any fighting developed, let it be on Polish, not Russian, soil! Meanwhile, he had bought valuable time—time he used to build Russian defenses at a frantic pace.

As Nazi divisions thundered into Poland, England and France felt compelled to declare war. If Hitler had forsworn an attack on Russia, it could only mean that he intended to turn west for new conquests. But on June 22, 1941, Hitler suddenly broke his pact with Stalin and sent massive Nazi armies storming across eastern Poland into the USSR.

Stalin rallied the Russian people, not in the name of Communism, but of Mother Russia. He called for a "scorched earth policy"—burning everything in retreat and leaving the conquerors only empty space. Working around the clock, he proved an inspiring tower of strength to his people. If they had once feared and hated him, now they trusted and obeyed him with great patriotic feeling.

He dismantled whole Soviet war industries in Hitler's path, reassembling them in the Ural Mountains beyond Moscow. He checked, blunted, and trapped the might of Hitler's powerful armies, sacrificing twenty million Russian dead to defend Moscow and Leningrad. He even made his peace with the Russian Orthodox Church to win their support of the Soviet war effort.

The terrible pressure of the Nazi offensive was relieved when Allied forces headed by General Dwight Eisenhower opened a Second Front in northern France on June 6, 1944. Germany, caught in the nutcracker squeeze between East and West, was finally crushed on May 7, 1945.

Russian occupations of Eastern Europe after the war worried President Harry Truman, who coldly disagreed with

Stalin's insistence that only pro-Soviet governments could now be tolerated between Berlin and Moscow. Stalin was furious when the Truman Doctrine began resulting in air bases being put all around the Soviet Union. The Cold War had begun.

Stalin sought a symbolic victory by blockading Berlin, an Allied land island within East Germany, to force the Western powers out. Truman thwarted him by a sensational airlift of forty-five hundred tons of supplies to Berliners every day. The political struggle united the Western powers in an anti-Soviet alliance, the North Atlantic Treaty Organization (NATO).

Stalin angrily struck back by encouraging the Communist government of North Korea in aggressive moves against the United States-supported South Koreans. Truman outwitted Stalin by winning United Nations military support for South Korea. The Korean War became the new arena for East-West rivalry in the Cold War.

In 1953, Stalin suddenly suffered a stroke. When he died on March 5, he was held in great awe and respect, but loved by few. "He was a great man," said British Labour Party leader Herbert Morrison, "but not a good man."

III. Nikita Khrushchev (1894–1971)

"We will bury you!" Nikita Khrushchev once snarled at a representative of the capitalistic United States he hated yet envied. He was born in a mud and reed hut on April 17, 1894, in a Ukrainian village so poor that only one man owned a pair of boots. His grandfather had been a serf who had had only two baths in his life—one at baptism, one at burial. His father was a farmer and part-time coal miner.

"My parents were *muzhiks,* poorest of the poor," he recalled. "We went hungry to bed most nights."

As a boy Nikita herded cows for a feudal lord, and was once caught fishing for supper in the estate pond. The gamekeeper flogged him with a lead-weighted leather whip, then dragged him to the police to be flogged again. At fifteen he went to work in the mines and ironworks of Yuzovka—"Dog Town" to the miners who lived there in huts and caves.

Rebellious, aggressive, rude, and impatient, he also had a more likable side, displaying a blunt sense of humor and a love of boisterous companionship that made him popular.

Ordered to crawl into hot boilers to clean them out, he almost burned alive on the hot bricks before scrambling to safety, black with soot and gasping for breath. "There I discovered something about capitalists," he said later. "All they wanted from me was the most work for the least money that would keep me alive. So I became a Communist. Life is a great school. It thrashes and bangs and teaches you!"

He was fired for leading a miners' protest, and his papers were afterward marked with a secret symbol warning other employers that he was a dangerous agitator. One May Day as he drank with friends, he became aware of a spy trailing him. He kept toasting the Tsar, and insisted that the spy join the group. When the spy passed out, dead drunk, the others sped off to run a red flag up the tallest smokestack in town to celebrate May Day.

Khrushchev was inspired by a Marxist poet who prophesied a revolutionary Russia in which the most wretched peasants would be educated into people of culture, capable of enjoying the world's greatest art, music, and books. This was his dream as he joined the Red Guards in the October Revolution of 1917.

"The old bad days are over!" he cried. "Now there are no more masters—only citizens!" The Communist Party sent him to a Yuzovka school for three years of Marxist education. Here he met and married one of his teachers, Nina Petrovna, with whom he had three children. Displaying a talent for tough,

Nikita Khrushchev. (*United Nations*)

shrewd leadership, he was made a local Party boss to coax and bully production out of Ukraine miners and farmers.

At harvest time, he transferred miners to the collective farms to help bring in the crops. When farming was slow, he transported peasants to help out in the mines. Some superstitious peasants feared "earth demons." Teaming them with seasoned miners, he soothed their fears: "The earth is our mother, and in the mine you are close to her heart!"

Once an opponent tried to shout him down at a local Party meeting. "Hold up your hands!" Khrushchev snarled at him. "Look, comrades—those are the hands of a shopkeeper, not of miners like ourselves. Who will you trust?"

He dissipated discontent by earthy peasant humor that forced angry workers to laugh; if that failed he used blustering threats. "If an appeal to the head doesn't work, try the other end," he advised other Party leaders. "Where there is no thought, there may be feeling!"

His success at driving men was so impressive that he was put in charge of building Stalin's great showplace, the Moscow subway. Using "shock brigades" of workers, he rushed it to completion in record time, at a heavy cost in accidents. He endeared himself further to Stalin by blistering attacks on the "miserable dwarfs" and "Fascist degenerates" of the Moscow Trials. "They lifted their hands against the greatest of all men," Khrushchev wrote in *Pravda,* "our friend, our wise leader, Comrade Stalin!"

By March 1939, he had become one of the top eight members of the Politburo, and was made boss of the Ukraine. During World War II he supervised the giant transfer of Ukrainian factories to the east, directed guerrilla warfare behind Nazi lines, and helped defend Stalingrad.

When Stalin died in March 1953, there was a period of "collective leadership" in the Kremlin, led first by Malenkov, then Bulganin. Nikita Khrushchev cannily bided his time behind the scenes, gathering real power into his own hands. By September, he was made First Secretary of the Party.

It took three years before the new leaders in the Kremlin dared attack the Stalinist creed they had inherited. But on February 25, 1956, in a secret session of the twentieth Party Congress, they made fiery speeches damning the dead tyrant Khrushchev had once called "the greatest of all men."

The cold, grim spirit of Stalinism began to melt in the Soviet Union, giving way to a new liberal climate, more consumer goods, greater freedom, increasing sounds of laughter. Khrushchev even visited Yugoslavia to admit to Tito that he (Tito) had been right to oppose Stalin. In high spirits during the visit, Khrushchev playfully challenged Mikoyan to an impromptu wrestling match, and the two Soviet chieftains rolled merrily around in the roadside dust.

Anti-Communists in Hungary, chafing at Soviet postwar control, decided that if Tito could get away with thumbing his nose at Moscow, so could they. Staging an uprising in Budapest, they demanded political freedom. But now Khrushchev's smile turned to a snarl, and he sent Soviet tanks to crush the rebellion. "When it comes to fighting imperialists," he shouted furiously, "we are *all* Stalinists!"

World opinion was outraged. Bulganin tried to force him to resign as Party Secretary: "We have seven votes, and you have only four." Khrushchev sneered, "In mathematics, two and two are four indeed, but politics are another matter!" Rallying his supporters, he ousted his rivals, and in March 1958, became sole dictator of the Soviet Union.

The accomplishments of the nation's space scientists delighted him, especially when Russia became first in space with a satellite, Sputnik. He felt enormous pride that he, a poor peasant boy, had risen to the top of a nation so technologically advanced that it had even beaten the powerful United States in the space race. He flew around Europe and Asia to win new friends for his regime.

Resourceful, brash, hard as nails, he used every shrewd peasant's trick to convince other nations they did not need any anti-Soviet alliance. Selling Communism as "the wave of the future," he used boasts to impress the backward; barnyard humor to cajole the rural; warm sociability to charm the diplomatic set; threats to frighten weak Western satellites; Marxist persuasion to keep Red leaders pro-Soviet, anti-Mao.

It was part of Khrushchev's fascination that his hosts never knew what to expect from him. In Denmark, taken on an agrarian tour, he contemptuously dismissed Danish farms as "too small." In Sweden he told a group of shipbuilders, "Though I am a Communist and an atheist, and do not believe in such things, I hope you will ask God to help you get your prices down so we can continue to buy your ships!"

He hinted to President Eisenhower that he wanted to settle East-West differences over Germany, so that they could follow a "coexistence policy" of sharing the world peacefully, with only friendly rivalry for the hearts, minds, and markets of the neutral nations. Invited to Washington in the fall of 1959, he became the first Soviet dictator ever to set foot on American soil. He was stunned by the industrial might, agricultural plenty, technological sophistication, and worker comfort he saw in America. All those cars!

Piqued, he snapped at Eisenhower, "It's foolishly wasteful to have so many cars taking road space with only one person occupying them. Apparently your people do not seem to like the place where they live—always going someplace else! We don't need cars because we enjoy our neighborhoods. . . . Of course your press will not report my criticism!"

He was astonished when the President called in reporters to let him sound off, and he was able to read his caustic comments about American life in the next morning's papers.

Proudly flaunting his peasant origins, he refused to wear formal dress to a White House dinner in his honor. He was suspicious of an offer to show him Washington by helicopter, until Eisenhower indicated he would be flying with him.

Touring the country, Khrushchev both angered and fascinated Americans by a brash display of Communist showmanship. Shown a capitalist accomplishment, he would sneer, "Only the grave can correct a hunchback!" Forbidden to visit Disneyland for fear of exposing him to a crackpot attack, he exploded, "What—do you have rocket-launching pads there?" Upon meeting Senator Lyndon Johnson, he snapped, "I know all about you. I have read all your speeches and I don't like any of them!"

He was outraged at a dinner where AFL-CIO leaders attacked him more bitterly than had any American capitalist he had met. The two American products that impressed him most were potato chips and cornflakes. "They are nutritious and tasty," he told Party leaders later. "And they are cheap. See to it that we have a crop increase in corn and potatoes!"

He ended his United States tour at Camp David, Maryland, in cordial private talks with Eisenhower. They agreed upon a four-power "summit meeting" in Paris to settle the German question, and he returned to Moscow glowing with the new "spirit of Camp David." Finding his Kremlin colleagues skeptical about his trip, he assured them it had been a Red triumph:

"While I was standing on the airfield in Washington and saying goodbye to America, the band played the Soviet anthem, and then the guns fired twenty-one salutes," he related proudly. "So I said to myself, 'That first salute is for Karl Marx, and the second salute for Engels, and the third for Lenin, and the fourth for His Majesty the Working Class.' You must admit that's not bad, comrades—not bad at all!"

Just before the Paris Conference, however, he was seriously embarrassed when a U-2 American spy plane was shot down over Russia on May 1, 1960. "This is the Eisenhower you trusted?" sarcastically demanded Party ideologist Mikhail Suslov.

Unnerved, Khrushchev tried to give the American President an excuse by suggesting he hadn't known about the U-2 flights. But Eisenhower admitted he had authorized the flights "to prevent another Pearl Harbor."

That left Khrushchev no alternative. At the Paris summit he denounced both Eisenhower and the United States, wrecking the conference by stalking out in a rage. Washington suspected he might have done so anyhow, because of a failure to get other Kremlin leaders to agree to a Berlin settlement.

United States-USSR relations began sliding downhill. In the fall of 1960, he showed up at the United Nations to denounce Secretary Dag Hammarskjöld for "pro-Western bias." Overplaying his hand, he took off one of his shoes and began banging it on the desk to drown out Hammarskjöld's reply. United Nations members were shocked at his manners.

When President John Kennedy succeeded Eisenhower, Khrushchev tried to force him to recognize the Soviet puppet state of East Germany. Failing, he angrily ordered the building of the Berlin Wall. Then in October 1962, he stealthily sought to cancel the advantage of America's long-range missiles by planting Soviet short-range missiles in Castro's Cuba. When Kennedy discovered what he was up to, Khrushchev defended his move by pointing to American missile bases in Turkey aimed at the Soviet Union.

Unmoved, Kennedy put the United States and USSR "eyeball to eyeball" by blockading Soviet ships from Cuba with the American Navy. Khrushchev glumly agreed to withdraw the missiles.

The following year he assured United States Secretary of Agriculture Orville L. Freeman that he was far more interested in Soviet prosperity than in any costly armaments race with the United States. Drawing a finger across his throat, he admitted, "I've got rockets up to here!"

The more he tried to reach accord with the United States, the more vehemently he was denounced by Red China as a traitor to world revolution. Stung, he tried to arrange a summit meeting of Communist nations to expel China from Marxist ranks. "The day you convene your so-called summit," Mao Tse-tung snapped angrily, "you will step into your grave!"

In 1964, the seventy-year-old Khrushchev suddenly faced a revolt in his own ranks. Fed up with his boorish peasant manners and impulsive behavior, a coalition of Bolshevik leaders accused him of a "cult of personality"—the same charge he had leveled at Stalin. Suslov charged him with twenty-nine serious mistakes, not the least of these his crude behavior at the United Nations—"harmful to the reputation of the Soviet Union."

Frightened, Khrushchev shouted a blustering defense of his policies. "You see, comrades," Suslov said, "it is quite impossible to talk to him." In a fit of pique Khrushchev yelled, "My ministers are a bunch of blockheads!" The Party Central Committee voted to replace him with a dual leadership by Leonid Brezhnev and Alexei Kosygin. Crestfallen, he retired to a four-room apartment near the Kremlin, becoming a neighbor of Molotov and Zhukov, two former leaders he had kicked out.

Ironically, Khrushchev's date of birth was removed from the official Communist Party calendar at the same time Josip Stalin's birthday was restored to it. Brezhnev and Kosygin also ordered Soviet historians to prepare a "slightly more balanced" evaluation of Stalin's role in developing the USSR. Only one thing remained unchanged—Soviet dictatorship, denying the Russian people a free choice of leaders.

"Dictatorship," wrote Mikhail Bakunin, a nineteenth-century anarchist, "can have only one aim: self-perpetuation."

He has yet to be proved wrong.

3

Italy

Benito Mussolini (1883–1945)

"In this age, instead of the reign of the masses, there must come the reign of one great leader!" Benito Mussolini thundered in 1921. "Only one man's brains, one man's will, can get the most out of the Italian people!"

He was born on July 29, 1883, at Dovia in Predappio, Italy, in the vineyard country of the Romagna. His Socialist father was a poor blacksmith, his mother a village schoolteacher. Although an extremely bright boy, he was expelled from two schools for knife fights. Always a leader, he ruled his followers by force, threat, and revenge.

Once, as his gang raided an apple orchard, a boy was hit by a shotgun blast. All the gang fled except Mussolini, who carried the wounded boy to safety. Next day he sought out the deserters, one by one, and beat them mercilessly.

Wandering among the castle ruins above Predappio, he liked to daydream about the glories of ancient Rome. One day his mother was frightened by shouting from his locked room. "It's all right, Mama," he laughed. "I was just practicing some speeches for the day when I am ruler of Italy!"

Seeking work in Switzerland, he slept under a bridge in Lausanne; and he was once so hungry that he snatched a sandwich out of the hand of an amazed Englishwoman. He worked as a laborer, errand boy, tutor, journalist, and secretary of a bricklayers' union. Influenced by exiled revolutionaries he met, he was often flung into jail as a labor agitator.

His piercing eyes, jutting jaw, fiery manner, flowing black bow tie, and wide-brimmed black hat made him a marked figure. In 1904 Mussolini was finally expelled from Switzerland as a chronic troublemaker. Returning home, he decided to marry. When his father objected, he flourished a gun and cried, "There are six bullets in it. If you don't consent to our marriage, one is for Rachele, and the other five are for me!"

He began seeking a political future by leading protest marches against unemployment and high prices. Once he threatened to throw the mayor out of the town hall window until that terrified official swore to lower the price of milk immediately.

The Forli Socialist Federation made Mussolini its secretary in 1910. Two years later, he won national prominence.

Becoming editor of the Socialist paper *Avanti!,* he wrote biting articles that tripled its circulation. At first he upheld the Socialists' anti-war, pro-revolutionary policy. But he suddenly reversed himself when the French government sent a secret emissary to bribe him into advocating Italy's entrance into World War I on the Allied side. The bribe was a newspaper which would be all his own—*Il Popolo d'Italia.*

Outraged Socialists denounced him as a turncoat and warmonger. Trying to defend himself at a mass meeting of Milan Socialists, he was stunned by furious cries of "Traitor! Judas! Hireling!" He shouted passionately, "I am and will always be a Socialist. You hate me only because you love me!"

When Italy entered the war, he was drafted and fought in the Alps on the Austro-Italian border. An accidental explosion of his trench mortar put forty-four pieces of steel into his body. Given up for dead, he gasped, "I *refuse* to die! Even if all the doctors explode with exasperation! I snap my fingers at medical science. It is my destiny to live!"

Benito Mussolini. (*U. S. Information Agency*)

Postwar Italy fell into a state of revolutionary chaos. Rejected by the Socialists, Mussolini sought a new way to capitalize on popular discontent. He organized jobless veterans, small businessmen, and underworld characters into the "Milan Fighters' Fascio," hailing them as "Italy's future supermen." Their destiny: to save the nation from Communists, Socialists, Catholics, Freemasons, Social Democrats, anarchists, and pacifists. He gave them a uniform of a black shirt and a beret, and a flag with a white skull on a black field.

Thundering against "the menace of Bolshevism" in *Il Popolo,* he led his private army in street brawls. "I fear no one," he boasted, "as long as I have a pen in my hand and a revolver in my pocket." He confided to a friend, "I'm obsessed with a wild desire to mark my era with my will, like a lion with a claw—so!" His nails ripped chair upholstery.

When he ran for a seat in the Chamber of Deputies, his followers organized torchlight parades, tossed bombs into Socialist meetings, beat up his opponents, and forced castor oil down their throats. By May 1921, the Fascists had grown so powerful that Mussolini was elected to Parliament along with thirty-three lesser "Blackshirts." Seeking total power, he made a deal with Italy's chief industrialists. In return for their support, he would destroy the labor unions.

In October 1922, he gave King Victor Emmanuel a blunt ultimatum: "Either the government must be handed over to us, or we shall seize it by marching on Rome!" The frightened monarch capitulated, but nevertheless Mussolini staged a showy march on Rome with his legions. Bursting into the Quirinal, he told the King dramatically, "Your Majesty must excuse my black shirt—I come fresh from the battlefield!"

Mussolini's rule began dynamically. He forced open factories shut by strikes, ordered trains to be run on time, kept farm crops moving to market, insisted upon efficient operation of government services, won a hundred-million-dollar loan from American banks.

Calling a special meeting of Parliament, he made clear his powers as combined Prime Minister, Home Secretary, and Foreign Minister. "I could have filled this dull, gray hall with corpses," he shouted. "I could have nailed up the doors of Parliament. You are sitting here only because of my generous gesture toward national unity. But my will to act must not be delayed for a second by useless oratory!" None dared protest.

Making balcony speeches to huge crowds, he excited them by flights of bombastic oratory. "We Fascists throw poisonous ideas about liberty on the rubbish heap!" he roared. "Italians are tired of liberty. They want and need Order, Authority, Discipline!" He showed off to them by driving racing cars at top speed, stunting in airplanes, fencing with aides, galloping on thoroughbreds.

Although he scoffed at voting as "a childish game," he held general elections in 1924 to prove that his dictatorship spoke for the Italian people. Breaking up rival meetings, Fascists squads terrorized the voters at the polls and stuffed the ballot boxes. After his "victory," he toured Italy in triumph.

The more the crowds roared their admiration of him, the more he scowled at them. "They're nothing but a herd of sheep," he declared contemptuously, "incapable of ruling themselves."

He isolated himself, lofty, imperious, a demigod.

Suddenly his henchmen blundered by murdering a popular deputy by the name of Matteoti who led the Socialist opposition. Public uproar almost swept the Fascists out of office. Frightened, Mussolini whined to his aides, "What do you expect me to do with a corpse under my feet?" But they stiffened his backbone, and a reign of terror silenced all anti-Fascists. By 1929, his power was absolute. Strikes were outlawed, criticism of "Il Duce" was made a jail offense.

Mussolini began building white granite monuments to himself—huge stadiums, public works, Fascist statuary—and was constantly photographed turning over the first spade of earth, naked to the waist. "In five years," he thundered, "Rome must appear wonderful to the whole world, enormous, orderly, and powerful, as she was in the days of the first Roman Empire!"

Fierce, heroic portraits of him blossomed everywhere on walls and buildings. "VIVA IL DUCE!" was painted on mountain cliffs. A superb showman, he staged great parades and spectacles, all skillfully designed to dramatize himself. He survived four assassination attempts.

Still an avowed atheist, Mussolini sought to reconcile Catholicism and Fascism by a Lateran Concordat recognizing Catholicism as the official religion of Italy. He even kissed the Pope's slipper. Soon afterward, when the Pope disagreed with him, he ordered brutal attacks on priests and churches.

His costly public works program began to bankrupt Italy. He simply slashed wages to less than ten cents an hour, making Italians the lowest paid workers in Europe. "Fortunately," he explained, "the Italian people are not yet accustomed to eating several times a day. Since they have a modest standard of living, they don't feel want and suffering very much."

An attendant followed him around with a portfolio of money so that he could dispense charity as the whim moved him. A personal bomber and warship remained within call to fly or sail him anywhere at a moment's notice. "Money is only important," he said loftily, "when you don't have power."

Meanwhile in Germany an imitator, Adolf Hitler, stormed his way to power as Europe's second dictator. The two strong men detested each other. From admiring Mussolini at first, Hitler grew to scorn him as "an inferior Mediterranean type," a blusterer without real power. Mussolini scoffed, "What a clown this Hitler is! He's quite mad."

In 1935 Mussolini sent troops into Ethiopia to take it as an Italian colony. "Julius Caesar once dominated the world!" he reminded his people. When the League of Nations failed to stop him, Ethiopia was taken at a cost of fifteen hundred Italian dead. "Too few sacrifices for our own good!" he fumed at his conquering general, Badoglio. "If you had moved faster, with heavier casualties, we would have had a more impressive performance—and an empire dignified by the shedding of a respectable amount of Italian blood!"

Upon the outbreak of civil war in Spain, he joined Hitler in helping Franco, a fellow Fascist. They used Spain for war practice and testing equipment. "Besides," Mussolini told his son-in-law Ciano, "if Italians aren't kept fighting, the lazy pigs grow soft. Hitler's lucky. Germans are born Nazis. But Italians have to be *made* into Fascists!"

In 1937, Mussolini was invited to Munich by Hitler, who stunned him with a powerful military display. He meekly agreed to a Rome-Berlin Axis that made him Hitler's junior partner. Now slavishly copying the dictator who had begun by imitating him, Mussolini taught his army to goose-step and began persecuting Italy's Jews. When King Victor Emmanuel protested, Mussolini threatened to kick him off the throne.

Hitler sought to force Italy to support all his warlike moves against the West. But Mussolini moved cautiously, hoping his German partner would not go too far in bluffing the democracies. Italy was in no position to fight a major war. When war loomed over Hitler's threat to Czechoslovakia, Mussolini hastily arranged a peace conference at Munich.

Acting as conciliator, he won enough concessions from England and France to pacify Hitler. But in March 1939, Hitler tore up the Munich agreement and took over Czechoslovakia. Mussolini knew then that war was inevitable. He told Hitler meekly that Italy would have to stay out.

Then, without his aid, the Nazis swept through Poland, conquered France and the Low Countries. Fearful that he would be denied a share of the spoils if he delayed any longer, Mussolini declared war on the Allies.

"The war will be over by September," he told Marshal Badoglio hopefully. "I need only a few thousand dead to sit at the peace conference as a belligerent." His decision quickly proved disastrous. When his army invaded Greece, it was chased out by the Greeks and had to be rescued by an irate Hitler's forces. Whole divisions of the Italian army meekly surrendered to British forces in North Africa.

"I'll get them to gallop into it!" Mussolini raged. "All the cowards need is beating, beating, and *more* beating!" But bombs began falling on Italy, as the Allied armies speared north from Africa to capture Sicily. Mussolini knew then that he had lost his gamble: his days were numbered.

"It's the 'law of contrariety,' Füehrer," he told Hitler. "There are times when everything in life goes exactly opposite from the way you plan!"

Now openly contemptuous of the weak dictator, Hitler flew into rages at him. Mussolini's humiliation was complete when Hitler took over command of Italy's crumbling defenses. The Fascist Grand Council denounced Mussolini as the author of Italy's woes. The King ordered his arrest. Imprisoned, he cut a woeful figure.

"The celebrated outthrust chin doesn't look very strong now," observed an Italian admiral. "Only three days before, this crumpled man had been the supreme power in the land."

The Italian people staged wild celebrations at being rid of their tyrant. In the fall of 1943, Marshal Badoglio led a new Italian government that switched sides in the war.

Needing Mussolini as a front for a puppet regime in the north of Italy, Hitler arranged a dramatic rescue of his fallen partner. A Nazi commando force flew to a mountain resort where Mussolini was being held, and snatched him off to Hitler's headquarters in East Prussia. But Il Duce was now only a hollow shell of his former self. His attempt to rally his people back to Fascism was a dismal failure.

Italian partisans, underground anti-Fascist guerrillas, began to take over northern Italy ahead of the advancing Allied armies. Fleeing toward the Swiss border in disguise, Mussolini was recognized and arrested. On April 28, 1945, he was executed by a firing squad. His corpse was taken to Milan and strung upside down by the heels in the city square where he had once shouted fiery phrases about the glories of Fascism to roaring crowds.

4

Turkey

Mustafa Kemal Atatürk (1881–1938)

He was a great man and he was a terrible man.

He freed Turkey from European colonialism—and burned alive tens of thousands of Greek civilians in Smyrna, pitching their charred bodies into the harbor. He brought Turkey out of the Middle Ages into the twentieth century—and lived a personal life of barbaric depravity. He preached democracy for Turkey—and ruled as an absolute dictator, torturing and hanging his opponents.

Born in the Turkish quarter of Salonika, Greece, in 1881, he had only a first name, Mustafa, as was the custom of the old Ottoman Turks. He won a second name, Kemal ("Perfection"), from his teachers, who were impressed with his brilliance as a student. His third name, Atatürk ("Father of Turks"), he awarded to himself as a dictator.

Mustafa Kemal was eight when his lumberman father died, leaving the family impoverished. But he told his mother proudly, "I am going to be somebody!" At twelve he entered a government military school. Cold, arrogant, highly intelligent, he dominated his schoolmates, but his supercilious manner offended them.

The Turkey of his youth was no longer the powerful Ottoman Empire that had once dominated the Near East and the

Balkans. Shrunken to a small, weak nation, known as "the sick man of Europe," Turkey was treated as a semi-colony by foreign powers, who forced it to yield humiliating concessions. The Sultan, a backward tyrant, lived in dread of radicals who wanted to modernize the country.

Kemal at twenty was so promising a military talent that he was sent to Harbiye, Turkey's West Point, near Constantinople. Like most young army officers, he despised the Sultan and the whole rotting fabric of the Ottoman Empire. He read forbidden books that opened up inspiring vistas of the glittering, sophisticated societies of Western Europe and America. Why, Kemal wondered, hadn't Turkey also become a modern nation with a good life for all its people?

He came to the conclusion that religion had kept the Turks in feudal bondage. "Islam is a dead thing," he insisted. "Was it not for the Caliphate, for Islam, for the priests and such-like cattle, that for centuries the Turkish peasant has fought and died in every climate? The Caliphate has bled us white for centuries!"

He was also influenced by Halide Edib, Turkey's first feminist, a slender, redheaded divorcée who dared campaign openly for equal rights for women in a land where they were compelled to wear veils, and were the serfs of all-powerful husbands. A nation in which the women were not emancipated, Kemal agreed, would never emancipate itself either.

In Constantinople, he relaxed from his studies by getting drunk and chasing after different women every night, including other men's wives. He remained an unscrupulous playboy all his life.

In 1906, the tall, handsome cadet was posted to Damascus as a cavalry captain. Here, for two years, he worked secretly with a revolutionary society known as the Young Turks. In 1908 they finally overthrew the old Sultan, replacing him with a puppet

Mustafa Kemal Atatürk. (*Turkish Information Office*)

cousin. General Enver Pasha became Turkey's real ruler. Kemal was angered by his pro-German policies.

"Turkey for the Turks!" Kemal snarled. "Those who compromise with foreign powers never make a revolution!"

Enver warily exiled the firebrand, now a colonel, to a field command. When World War I broke out, Kemal urged neutrality, but Enver took Turkey into the war on Germany's side. Indignant but patriotic, Kemal quickly distinguished himself by repulsing a powerful British naval attack. Seizing the heights above Gallipoli, he led attacks on the beachheads.

"When you see me raise my hand," he shouted to his men, "fix bayonets and follow me!" For three months of bloody fighting, they threw back every enemy attempt to scale the cliffs. The frustrated British regiments finally gave up and were evacuated.

"Seldom in history did the exertions of a single commander," admitted the official British historian, "exercise so profound an influence on the fate of a campaign, and even the destiny of a nation."

Now a national hero, Kemal was promoted to general, but he continued his outspoken opposition to Germany. Turks, Kemal insisted, should fight for Turkey alone. When the Enver government finally fell in the German defeat of November 1918, Kemal refused to disband his troops. Defying both a new Sultan and British forces occupying Constantinople, he established a rebel government in Anatolia.

He had Soviet help. "Of course Mustafa Kemal is no Socialist," Lenin admitted, "but he's a good organizer, a talented military man, a man of progressive inclinations, and a wise statesman. He's carrying out a bourgeois national revolution, and a war of liberation against aggressors."

The Sultan put a price on Kemal's head. In the bloody civil war that followed, both sides flogged, tortured, crucified, and hanged prisoners.

In 1920, Kemal set up a National Assembly in Ankara. His leadership was challenged by rivals who denounced his savage tongue, his cruelty, his drunkenness, his blasphemy against holy Islam. But his fame as a military hero, nationalist, and patriot was too great to deny him election as president of the new rebel government.

He launched an attack on Constantinople to throw the British out of Turkey. They sent a powerful Greek army of a hundred thousand men against him. His troops panicked and ran.

Ordering hundreds of deserters shot, Kemal raged at his army, "We are Turks—we will never be the subjects of a people who only yesterday were our slaves!" His men, as frightened of him as of the Greeks, turned and fought desperately. "Not one inch of Turkish soil will be surrendered," he thundered, "until it is drenched in Turkish blood!"

Promoting himself from president to generalissimo, he decisively routed the Greek Army in 1922, driving them into the sea by the thousands. He sneered at wretched Greek prisoners: "Here you see the centuries of progress made by that wonderful animal, man!" The British position in Turkey was now hopeless. Returning to Ankara, Kemal was awarded the title of "Ghazi" ("Victorious"), and given dictatorial powers subject to renewal by the Assembly every three months.

At the Peace Conference in Versailles, his military victories forced the Allies to impose only mild peace terms on Turkey as a defeated German ally. The Sultan was deposed and Turkey became a republic.

Elected its first President in 1923 by a hand-picked Assembly, Kemal promptly abolished all special rights of foreign powers and ordered the British to get out of Turkey. When they tried to bribe him, he snapped, "Kemal is not for sale!"

With Turkey free of domination at last, he set about transforming his country from a backward Oriental slum into a modern nation. Although he hated all Western powers, he respected the twentieth-century techniques that had made them great. In order to sweep aside all opponents of progress, he turned his presidency into an absolute dictatorship.

He grew furious at those who tried to compare him to Mussolini: "I am no hyena in jackboots, no political gangster!"

He abolished the Caliphate, separated church and state, and took education out of the hands of the priests. The Caliph himself was kicked out of Turkey unceremoniously; two days later all Ottoman royalty was thrown out after him. An Assembly delegate who dared protest was promptly murdered.

The faithful of Islam were stirred against Kemal. Many conservative Turks were appalled by his private life, especially when he divorced his wife and discarded a mistress, who then committed suicide. Kemal found himself becoming tremendously unpopular. Several attempts were made on his life. Soon it was so dangerous for him to appear in public that traffic had to be cleared off any road on which he planned to drive.

Nevertheless, he persisted with his reforms. Factories and industries sprang up, financed by foreign loans. He introduced free education, and abolished the Arabic alphabet so as to spread literacy through use of the easier Roman alphabet. He divided two million acres of church land among Turkish peasants, and turned mosques into granaries.

The fez was abolished, and his police saw to it that only Western hats appeared on the street. Photos of Kemal himself in white tie and tails were published to discourage old Turkish dress. Banning Muslim veils, he insisted that Turkish women "show their faces to the world." He urged them to wear short skirts and high heels like Western women. "A nation cannot progress without its women," he declared, and gave them the right to vote, hold jobs, and own property. He appointed women judges, banned polygamy, permitted divorces for women.

Western music, studies, and legal codes were introduced. Swamps were drained, vaccination made compulsory. Insisting that all Turks must take second names so as to be even more like Westerners, he called himself Kemal Atatürk—justifiably.

"He was father of a reborn nation," observed author John Gunther, "at once a ruthless psychopath and a patriotic colossus. He picked up Turkey like at mangy dog and shook it into shape." He even shifted the capital from Asiatic Constantinople (Istanbul) to the new European city of Ankara.

The message to Turks was loud and clear. Everything Asian was wretched; everything Western was admirable. Atatürk drove the point home in an Assembly speech that lasted an incredible six days. Some grumbled that he was less interested in creating a new nation than in egotistically impressing his will upon Turkey. Halide Edib, the Turkish suffragette, revealed that, when argued with, he became "brutally clear and frank." He once told her bluntly, "What I mean is this: I want everyone to do as I wish and command!" She was thoroughly disillusioned when he executed some of her closest friends for "treason."

Isolated from his supporters by the typical paranoiac distrust of a dictator, he grew increasingly lonely. In fits of depression he would suddenly leave a drunken party, jump into a fast car at dawn, and speed off, vanishing for days at a time.

By 1930, Turkey was boiling with discontent. Atatürk decided it might be wise to let the opposition blow off some steam in the Assembly. He ordered a few deputies to speak and vote *against* him. Terrified, they begged him not to put them in this position, fearful he meant to use such token opposition as a pretext for hanging them.

"I'll hang you if you *don't*" he threatened.

It was a tactical mistake. The Turkish people, hearing open criticism of Atatürk in the Assembly, concluded that he no longer had dictatorial powers. The nation exploded in widespread strikes and rioting. A religious fanatic in Smyrna began gathering an army to overthrow the "atheist republic." Atatürk promptly hung thirty of the religious insurgents, and clamped the lid on any more dissent. "I can make Turkey a democracy if I can live another fifteen years," he said to an aide. "If I die it will take three generations!"

On November 10, 1938, the dictator died of cirrhosis of the liver. Only then did his people, looking around at the new Turkey he had built for them, begin to think well of their tyrant.

If his accomplishment was impressive, it was far from all-embracing. Three decades after his death, the well-dressed, well-housed, well-fed middle class of the Turkish cities was still only a small minority of the population. Most Turks were still illiterate peasants barely subsisting on about nine dollars a month. Only one village in fifty had electricity. The peasants used iron-spiked sticks for plows, and most transportation was by horse or mule. The national economy was stagnant. Democracy was fitful and impermanent; army coups overthrew presidents regularly.

But perhaps Atatürk did more than any other dictator of his time to liberate his country from foreign domination and bring it out of the dark ages. Largely because of his teaching, Turkey remained neutral during World War II.

"Turkey for the Turks!" Atatürk had cried.

His people never forgot it.

5

China

"Let China sleep," said Napoléon. "When it wakes, the world will be sorry." Certainly by the 1960s, an aroused Red China had few friends, either among the democracies or among the dictatorships of the Communist world.

With a recorded history of four thousand years, China is one of the oldest civilized countries. It considered all foreign nations as barbarian until 1839, when the Emperor of China felt compelled to go to war with Britain to stop the corruption of his people through the use of India-grown opium. Losing the war, he was forced to yield Hong Kong to the British and open Chinese ports to Western trade. By 1900, all imperialist powers were scrambling for profits in China. The resultant Open Door Policy provoked hatred of foreigners among the Chinese people.

Young patriots called the Boxers, not unlike the Red Guards of Communist China in 1967, staged government-inspired riots to drive the foreigners out. However, when the armed forces of eight invading powers repelled them, their tyrannical, backward Manchu rulers stood helplessly by.

The Chinese people turned to a new nationalist force, the Kuomintang ("National People's Party"), whose leader Dr. Sun Yat-sen, promised "nationalism, democracy, welfare of the people." In 1911 the Kuomintang overthrew the Manchu dynasty. To prevent civil war, Sun Yat-sen agreed to recognize the warlords' control of their regions, in return for their support of a

Republic of China. When a new Russia also emerged from the ruins of an overturned tsarist dynasty, Sun sought Soviet help in building a Nationalist Army.

Chinese-Soviet cooperation made allies of Chiang Kai-shek, a brilliant young career officer under Dr. Sun, and Mao Tse-tung, a Communist leader. Chiang held power in South China; Mao in North China. Their alliance lasted until the death of Sun Yat-sen in 1925, when they became bitter enemies.

I. Chiang Kai-shek (1887–1975)

Stubborn and cruel, Chiang executed thousands of Chinese for the crime of disagreeing with him. General Josip Stilwell, his American Chief of Staff during World War II, dubbed him contemptuously "a peanut dictator." He added that Chiang was "a grasping, bigoted, ungrateful little rattlesnake."

Chiang Kai-shek was born in the Chekiang Province in 1887, son of a village merchant. He prepared for a military career at a North China military academy and a Japanese staff college. He was fifteen when his family arranged a marriage for him to a neighbor's daughter, whom he divorced nineteen years later. Joining the Japanese Army, he admired its rigid discipline, but deserted in 1911 to join Dr. Sun's revolution in China. With incongruous courtesy, he mailed back his Japanese sword and uniform.

Chiang became a major general of the Kuomintang armies, but was unable to control the Chinese warlords. In 1923, Sun Yat-sen arranged for him to go to Moscow to learn Soviet military methods, and to get Kremlin help in setting up an officer-training academy near Canton. Stalin also agreed to order Chinese Reds to join the Kuomintang.

When Dr. Sun died in 1925, Chiang became Commander-in-Chief of the Nationalist Army. Setting out to unify China by military conquest, he forced the warlords in the north to bow to his authority. Changsha, Wuchang, Hankow, and other key centers quickly fell to him. But he brooded over the dangerous popularity of Mao Tse-tung, who was leading landless peasants against rich landlords, workers against industrialists.

In 1927 powerful Chinese and foreign business interests in Shanghai offered him full financial support for the Kuomintang, if he agreed to wipe out the Communists. Without warning, he attacked the Red Chinese stronghold in Shanghai, slaughtering thousands of workers. He extended the massacre to Nanking and Canton. Denunciation came from his own son, who fled to the Soviet Union in shocked dismay.

All Leftist elements withdrew from the Kuomintang. Pulling back to Kiangsi Province, they set up the first Chinese Soviets. The country fell into civil war between Communists and Nationalists. The warlords Chiang had sworn to overthrow now hailed him as their champion. To add to his respectability, he wooed and won beautiful Mei-ling Soong, Wellesley-educated daughter of the rich Soong family of Canton. Soon afterward he was baptized a Christian.

To win the Chinese people away from Mao, he used funds made available by the Shanghai financiers to expand cotton crops, develop rural health services, build a few hydraulic factories, and start a network of motor roads. He introduced the "New Life Movement," a curious state cult blending sanitation, Christianity, and Confucianism, and urged the Chinese people to imitate the Japanese in accepting national discipline. His feeble efforts at social reform barely scratched the surface of China's ancient ills.

Instead of attacking the warlords, he persuaded them to "repent their sins" and atone by making donations to the Kuomintang treasury. Pardoned, they were allowed to continue their despotic rule of their provinces. To allay discontent among the masses, Chiang used the Communists as scapegoats,

Chiang Kai-shek and his wife. (*Hamilton Wright*)

representing his civil war against them as a holy crusade. Blue Shirts, his secret police, terrorized Red Army sympathizers.

In 1931, Japan took advantage of the civil war to invade and colonize Manchuria. The threat to the rest of China was unmistakable. Chiang's aides begged him to reconcile with Mao for a joint struggle against the Japanese.

"No!" he raged. "The Japanese are only a disease of the skin. The Communists are a disease of the heart!" Some of his best officers were reported to have expressed suspicions that he was pro-Japanese. He had them executed.

For the next three years, ignoring the Japanese in Manchuria, he launched a campaign of "annihilation" against the Red Army. In October 1934, he succeeded in driving them out of their Kiangsi Soviet to the northwest of China.

Three years later, the Japanese prepared to spear south from Manchuria. In ten days they killed almost a million Chinese in Nanking, and ordered Chiang to surrender. The glum dictator flew to Sian to confer with the "Young Marshal" Chang Hsuehliang. He suddenly found himself seized and held prisoner.

"You must stop fighting civil wars," young Chang insisted. "There must be a common defense with Mao against Japan. You have lost a sixth of China without firing a shot. All you do is chase and murder peasants!"

Outraged, Chiang refused to eat, talk, or listen.

"Which are you, my subordinate or my enemy?" he roared. "If my subordinate, you should obey my orders. If you are my enemy, you should kill me without delay . . . I would rather sacrifice my life than compromise my principles!"

Madame Chiang flew to Sian in a bold attempt to plead personally for her husband's life. In an even more dramatic development, Chou En-lai, Mao's chief aide, arrived unexpectedly at Sian to argue eloquently for a total Chinese effort against the Japanese. Knowing that he had lost face badly, Chiang sullenly agreed and was set free.

The uneasy alliance of Mao and Chiang kept the Japanese from taking over their country. Then in January 1941, Chiang issued secret orders for a Kuomintang attack on the Red Fourth Army. Mao's forces suffered ten thousand casualties. When Mao protested bitterly, Chiang professed to be grieved that anyone would lay the blame for "the errors and failings of subordinates" at his honorable door.

When World War II broke out, Chiang angered even his own lieutenants by hoarding American war supplies, given to him to use against the Japanese, for use against Mao. President Roosevelt assigned General "Vinegar Joe" Stilwell as Chiang's "Chief of Staff." Stilwell, whose real mission was to supervise the proper use of United States military aid, fumed at Chiang as an "obstinate, pigheaded, ignorant, arbitrary, unreasonable, illogical" dictator.

Chiang issued secret orders to his officers to disregard Stilwell's commands, and pretended to be puzzled by his generals' "foolish" failure to cooperate. Their loyalty to him was assured by the corruption of his regime. They were getting rich by smuggling opium, gas, and cloth into wartime China. Even the Chinese Red Cross was used as a racket to steal and sell medicines. Army food was sold on the black market. Only poor Chinese who could not afford bribes were drafted.

Understandably, whole companies of Kuomintang soldiers began to desert to the Red Army. Once Mao's forces returned over one hundred rifles to the Nationalists with a note: "We can't force your men to return, but here are their arms."

Chiang preserved face by permitting no one to speak before he did, to argue, or to ask questions. Madame Chiang was even more imperious in her many roles as adviser, translator, diplomat, even commander of his air force. "Not only God," she once wrote cynically, "but everybody else is on the side of the big battalions." She told Stilwell she would have him made a four-star general if he backed up her demand for more aid to the Kuomintang during a trip she planned to Washington.

The trip did not prove an unqualified success.

"When she came to my New York apartment, she couldn't believe I had no butler," Mrs. Eleanor Roosevelt related. "She had expected the ménage of a reigning monarch, I think." Presidential secretary William Hassett said, "Madame will long be remembered . . . as arrogant and overbearing, . . . The concensus is that she is temperamental. All attempts to get her out of the country have failed—which is a break for the Generalissimo!"

Chiang's own diplomacy was even less tactful. At the Cairo Conference in November 1943, his arrogant demands exasperated General George Marshall. The United States Army Chief of Staff burst out, "Now let me get this straight. You are talking about your 'rights.'. . . I thought these were *American* planes, and *American* personnel, and *American* materiel. I don't understand what you mean that *we* can or can't do thus and so!"

Frustrated, Chiang took out his rage in petty tirades against subordinates. At graduation exercises of the Chinese Military Academy, he screamed at the band leader for a sour note. When a flustered official miscued an announcement, Chiang bawled out furiously, "Shoot him! Shoot him!"

A United States White Paper on China revealed that the Generalissimo had received five billion dollars' worth of American planes, tanks, and guns during the war. Hoarding most of this until the war was over, Chiang flung his Nationalist Army of three million against Mao's million troops. The Red Army fought largely with weapons captured from the Japanese.

Stilwell's disgust with Chiang led to his recall home. "What will the American people say," he wrote to his wife, "when they finally learn the truth?" But the War Department swore him to secrecy. Even after his death in 1946, it took two years before his revelations could be published.

Most of the Chinese people saw Mao's Red Army as liberators from Kuomintang brutality, taxes, robbery, and indifference to their suffering and poverty. Only a missionary friend,

Dr. George Shepherd, dared rebuke Chiang for letting his troops treat Chinese peasants worse than the Reds treated landlords. But the Generalissimo's troops, too, were becoming disillusioned. As corrupt commanders pocketed company payrolls, unpaid Nationalist soldiers sold their rifles to Mao's troops.

Many went over to the Red Army. By 1947, Chiang's defeats had cast doubt on his claim that the Kuomintang had "a mandate from Heaven" to rule China. The people were further antagonized by widespread arrests and assassinations of intellectuals by his Blue Shirt terrorists.

Troubled, President Truman reproached Chiang for encouraging "the selfish interests of extremist elements." The Generalissimo replied blandly, "Of course, mistakes have been made by some subordinates on the government side," but he insisted the Reds were worse. Truman wrote, "The Generalissimo's attitude and actions were those of an old-fashioned warlord . . . there was no love for him among the people."

By 1948, the Red Army had won all of Manchuria and defeated Chiang in a decisive battle near Hsuchow. A year later, his position hopeless, he was forced to flee to Formosa.

There he remained plotting futilely to return to the mainland and retake China for the Kuomintang. With the aid of the United States, which for political reasons continued to recognize his regime as the only legal government of China well into the 1970s, he modernized and brought prosperity to Formosa. But between 1957 and 1962 he spent one and a half million dollars of United States foreign aid funds to hire American press agents and lobbyists. They helped him prevent recognition for Red China, and win some United States "hawk" support in Congress for his dreams of reconquering it.

"If when I die I am still a dictator," he once declared, "I will certainly go down into the oblivion of all dictators. If, on the other hand, I succeed in establishing a truly stable foundation for a democratic government, I will live forever in every home in China."

He never got a second chance.

II. Mao Tse-tung (1893–1976)

Riding mules past a cluster of landlords' heads dangling from a tripod in the dirt street, the two Red Army men wore simple peak caps, sweat-stained coarse tunics, and no insignia of rank. But they were both important men, worth a hundred thousand dollars dead or alive to Chiang Kai-shek. Mao Tse-tung, forty-one, had long black hair and deep-set eyes set in a round, flat face. The other soldier was his chief military aide, burly Chu Teh.

The whistle of bombs cut through the afternoon haze. The two men plunged beside a wall as the street exploded in a maelstrom of blood and dust. Men, women, children ran screaming in all directions. A stick of high explosives bracketed a nearby tavern as Nationalist pilots dove on Ningtu. Mao bounced two feet in the air as the tavern collapsed in huge columns of dust. Smoke belched upward amid yellow flashes, releasing an earthy, sour smell from the walls.

"The time has come to leave Kiangsi Province," Mao told Chu. "But we will leave Chiang only scorched earth."

It was October 1934. Daily air assaults were smashing the Red bastion in Kiangsi to rubble. Now children worked night and day beside their parents to dismantle small factories and load the parts on mules and donkeys, along with food, arms, and silver bullion. Under cover of night about a hundred thousand Red soldiers and civilians left Kiangsi.

Mao and Chu marched at their head. Their goal was the distant Communist province of Shensi, where Mao planned to regroup and fight a guerrilla war against the Japanese. Hiding by day to avoid Chiang's observation planes and encounters with his army, they marched only at night.

"Enemy advances, we retreat," Mao told his aides. "Enemy escapes, we harass. Enemy retreats, we pursue. Enemy tires, we attack. We must take two steps forward, one back."

With him on the Long March went his pregnant second wife, twenty-four-year-old Ho Tzu-ch'un, and their four children. His first wife and sister had been executed in Chiang's massacre of Shanghai workers seven years earlier.

The Red Army's year-long journey on foot took them over six thousand miles through roaring gorges, over glaciers, into poisonous marshes, across terrain so wild no man had ever set foot there before. Less than one in five survived the daily battles against dive-bombers, Chiang's infantry, fierce triblesmen, starvation, disease, and terrible cold.

The leader of this famous Long March was born in Hunan Province in 1893, son of a poor peasant. His father had prospered, however, by acquiring land and making his family slave long hours on little food. Once he had denounced Mao before guests as a lazy, useless boy. Replying insolently, Mao had fled to a pond, threatening to drown himself if his father tried to beat him. His mother saved him by getting him to kneel at his father's feet in a humble apology.

"I learned to hate him," Mao recollected. "Never so much, perhaps, as when he sent me to school with landlords' sons. They all wore expensive clothes and treated me like a servant because my father—the miser!—kept me there in one ragged suit, without a penny."

He was ordered to study only the classics, which could aid his father in winning lawsuits. Mao rebelliously read all the forbidden books he could get his hands on. He was inspired by two heroes of history—Washington and Napoléon.

Working in the Peking University library led him to distrust Buddhism, the Manchu dynasty, and all the old ways of China.

Mao Tse-tung. (*Wide World Photos*)

He joined the student revolutionary movement, and became a leader in organizing the Chinese Communist Party. Using captured weapons, the Party began to exercise control in parts of China where the Kuomintang was most hated.

Hiding in the mountains, Mao developed techniques of fighting guerrilla warfare. "The people are like the water," he explained. "We must swim among them like fish. We must first learn from the masses, and then teach them." He relied upon the peasantry for support, concealment, food, and enlistments. "Armament is not the important factor in war," he said. "Man is." Chiang held the opposite view.

For the first month of the Long March, the Red Army stumbled along in pitch blackness, often in drenching downpours that did not stop by dawn. Struggling through a world of yellow mud, they exhausted their strength by half-pushing, half-pulling the stubborn mules. To move faster Mao ordered surplus machine guns, machinery, and even silver bullion dumped off the mules and buried. Lin Piao, a one-eyed Red leader, protested bitterly.

"If you need any of these things," Mao replied, "take them from Chiang's troops. Let *them* be our supply corps."

The columns wound up, down, and around hills like a fifty-mile-long Chinese dragon. On the thirty-fourth day, the Red Army took Schuicheng. Mao ordered its landlords to dig up the grain they had hidden. Those who refused were dragged to the public square and put "on trial." Some were only small landowners denounced by neighbors who wanted their land. Forced to kneel and surrender title deeds to their lands, they were then turned over to the peasants to be brutally murdered.

Approximately a hundred twenty-five thousand Chinese landowners were executed in this fashion. Taxed with these crimes in later years, Mao said, "To put it bluntly, it was necessary to bring about a brief reign of terror. To right a wrong, you must exceed the proper limits."

On the 103rd day of the Long March, his wife was hurt in a raid by Chiang's dive-bombers. Mao doctored her wounds with herbal medicines, then left their three smallest children behind at a nearby peasant's hovel for safekeeping.

"We will never see them again!" his wife wept.

Nor did they. Mao calmly told his wife, "Three seeds are as nothing in a forest of four hundred thousand trees."

They came to the raging Tatu River in a steep gorge on the 206th day. To reach a suspension bridge sixty miles away, Mao led his followers single file along slippery gorge walls. They continued to move only at night, a weird procession lit by ten thousand yellow torches. Frozen in the icy damp, exhausted marchers collapsed, slipping into the roaring depths below.

Mao gave away his coat to one freezing wounded soldier, an act for which he was glorified in Red Chinese textbooks for children. He had spent a lifetime toughening himself for just such ordeals. As a young man he had gone without food for days, swum in icy waters, walked shirtless in snow and sleet, marched across the ice of the Gulf of Pei in the dead of winter. This steeliness in his nature made him an austere, dedicated fanatic ready to sacrifice millions of lives, if need be, for a Red China.

Reaching the suspension bridge, Mao found it had been destroyed by Nationalist troops who were dug into a machine-gun nest on the opposite bank. Volunteers swung hand over hand from chain cables still intact. Dozens of them were shot into the gorge until one soldier managed to hurl a grenade accurately before plunging to his death. The Red Army laid bamboo on the cables and crossed.

On June 1, 1935, they climbed up to windswept Ma An-shan Pass, ten thousand feet above sea level. Some women, too weak to resist, were blown away down the mountain. Other marchers lay down in the snow to rest and never rose again.

With five more ranges still to cross, on the 251st day Mao, sick with fever, began to stagger. The marchers struggled through waist-deep mud that swallowed the last of their pack animals. As they wound through a narrow mountain defile, boulders came crashing down, hurled by Mantzu tribesmen whose queen boiled alive any Mantzu caught helping the Reds.

By the 341st day they were eating grass roots, chewing on hides, and dying of starvation. As they stumbled out of marshy grasslands, they were suddenly attacked by Nationalist troops and Muslim cavalry—Chiang's last attempt to destroy them before they could reach sanctuary.

Mao called upon his followers for one last gigantic act of endurance. Thousands of Reds were slaughtered, but they smashed a hole through the Kuomintang forces and escaped. On October 20, 1935, the Long March finally ended as twenty thousand survivors staggered into Shensi.

The Chinese people regarded with awe the leader who had led the Red Army through fifteen major battles and three hundred skirmishes, across eighteen mountain ranges and twenty-four rivers, through six wild aboriginal tribe lands, for one year and six days.

"However one may feel about the Chinese Reds and what they represent politically," said American journalist Edgar Snow, "it is impossible to deny recognition of their Long March . . . as one of the great exploits of military history. Hannibal's march over the Alps looks like a holiday excursion beside it!" It was to recapture this same revolutionary spirit of his Long March that, thirty years later, Mao threw Red China into virtual civil war against other Red leaders he felt were growing too soft, bourgeois, and conciliatory.

In the ten years when he kept his ragged followers living in mud huts and mountain caves at Yenan, Mao had warned against trusting any of the bourgeoisie. "Political power," he wrote, "comes out of the barrel of a gun!"

When World War II forged an alliance between the United States, the Soviet Union, and China, he agreed to collaborate with Chiang against Japan. He won tremendous prestige by keeping the Red Army a disciplined force that treated the peasantry well and fought brilliant guerrilla actions.

After the war they were so short of arms that, when Chiang turned on Mao, they had to set off firecrackers in gas tins to sound like machine guns. But Mao had a super-weapon Chiang did not—the support of the peasantry.

"Our goal is what Lincoln fought for in your Civil War—the liberation of slaves," he told an American reporter. "In China today we have millions of slaves, shackled by feudalism. Over eighty per cent of our people are peasants living on small plots of land belonging to unscrupulous landlords who enslave them by taking over half their food for rent."

The Red Army finally drove Chiang into exile on Formosa in 1949, and China was proclaimed a people's republic with Mao as its Chairman. Breaking up large land holdings, he distributed them among peasant tenants. During a visit to Moscow, he won Stalin's aid in developing Red China industrially.

As the power struggle between Stalin and the United States developed into war in Korea, Mao watched suspiciously from the sidelines. He became convinced that the West meant to use Korea to attack China, and sent Red Army "volunteers" to help the North Koreans. In the bitter fighting his own son, a fighter pilot, was shot down by the Americans.

With Stalin's death in 1953, Mao was faced with a new dilemma.

Khrushchev, the new Soviet leader, was denouncing Stalin and urging a new coexistence policy with the capitalistic West. To Mao this was a betrayal of the Marxist-Leninist doctrine of world revolution. Denouncing Moscow, he urged other Communist nations to follow Red China instead.

In imitation of Stalin, he sought to make China a first-class power by a sudden "Great Leap Forward"—a Five-Year Plan that threw a half billion Chinese into a frantic attempt to industrialize their nation, using even backyard furnaces. When it failed, Mao bitterly blamed Moscow: "Russia broke its agreements and pulled out its technicians in twenty-four hours, and they took all their blueprints with them." Droughts, floods, and mismanagement added to his difficulties.

Mao grew increasingly belligerent as he watched the United States ring Red China with military bases. "We aren't afraid of atomic bombs," he told a visiting Yugoslav diplomat in 1957. "What if they killed even three hundred million Chinese? We would still have plenty more. We will have our own atom bombs—and China would be the last country to die!"

He bitterly attacked the United States-Soviet nuclear test ban treaty of 1963 as "a swindle concluded behind our backs." Three years later he startled the world by successfully testing Red China's own missile-borne A-bombs.

Mao sought to win leadership of the Communist world away from Moscow, and to turn neutral nations against America. He tried to frighten India by an attack on its borders; invaded Tibet; plotted a Communist coup in Indonesia; sought to plant Red Chinese influence in Africa; encouraged guerrilla warfare in Vietnam. His aggressive foreign policy not only failed dismally, but increased Red China's isolation from the rest of the world.

Other top Red Chinese leaders began to insist that his policy was wrong, while that of the Soviet Union was right. Mao could not tolerate such "treason." A dictator must always be infallible. He sought to purge the Party of all except true believers. To rekindle the revolutionary spirit of the Long March, he sent youthful Red Guards swarming through the country in an often violent "cultural purge."

While the basic principle of the Cultural Revolution, as it came to be known, was the right to question those in charge, it ended up producing a mass cult of personality devoted to Mao. His little red book—a collection of *Quotations from Chairman*

Mao—became required reading for every man, woman and child in China.

During the early years of the movement, President Liu and other communist leaders were removed from power. Many were beaten and imprisoned. In the cities, the Red Guard splintered into competing groups that battled for dominance, and the bitter power struggle became open civil war in 1967 when Mao sent in army troops to restore order. As a result, the Chinese economy disintegrated with industrial production falling more than ten per cent from pre Cultural Revolution levels.

Amid the chaos, rifts opened at the top of the Communist Party, and these struggles marked the end of Mao's remaining years as his possible successors battled for control. In response, Mao militarized the party, dispatching soldiers to take control of schools, factories and government agencies. Then, he purged the military after claiming that his popular Minister of National Defense, Lin Biao, had attempted to assassinate him. These petty power struggles left many in China disillusioned with the tremendous sacrifices of the Cultural Revolution.

While the Cultural Revolution in the strict sense came to a close in 1969, many historians feel that it did not end until Mao's death in 1976. In its wake, it left over half a million people dead and millions more imprisoned, beaten and humiliated. The Communist Party had been decimated, and the people had lost much faith in their government. It is arguable that never before has a leader unleashed more destruction against the system that brought him to power—a fitting image for a leader with a legacy as ambivalent as Mao Tse-tung's.

6

Caribbean

The tragedy of the Caribbean island nations, like that of most of Latin America, was that for centuries most remained feudal societies with a handful of rich enslaving masses of poor. Lacking a stable middle class to work for democracy and reforms through honest elections, these nations continued to be powder kegs of revolution and dictatorship.

Equally tragic, the rich resources of the Caribbean have been plundered by racketeering dictators, in collusion with some American big-business interests. Presidents Wilson, Franklin Roosevelt, Eisenhower, and Kennedy have criticized the United States record of "dollar diplomacy"—supporting Latin-American dictators. Often this support has been urged and given under the guise of fighting Communism.

President Eisenhower admitted that he had been reluctant to withdraw support from Dominican Republic dictator Trujillo for fear a Communist government might replace him. When Santo Domingo erupted in civil warfare in April 1965, President Johnson rushed over twenty thousand troops to the island "to protect American nationals." Later he admitted that his real reason had been fear of a Communist coup.

For years, right-wing Latin-American dictators counted on that fear.

DOMINICAN REPUBLIC
Rafael Trujillo (1891–1961)

The thirty-one-year dictatorship of Rafael Trujillo turned a whole country into a private feudal estate, with the people enslaved to enrich Trujillo and his family. He entrenched himself in power by paying millions of dollars to American press agents and Washington lobbyists for a favorable image.

He was a mulatto, proud of his white ancestry, despising his dark Haitian inheritance. After working as an errand boy and cowhand, he joined a gang of juvenile delinquents who taught him the fine points of robbery, blackmail, and violence. He was twenty-four when United States Marines seized the bankrupt Dominican Republic on behalf of American investors, after which they governed it for nine years.

In 1918, after six months in jail for forgery, Trujillo worked for the Marines as a spy, betraying Dominicans opposed to the American occupation. He served the Marines so well that, when they trained a new Dominican army, he was made its general. The Marines finally left in 1929, after installing General Horacio Vásquez as President. Trujillo bided his time.

When Vásquez sought to remain in office beyond a four-year term, Trujillo cried indignantly, "Above all, I am against dictators!" His troops dispersed Vásquez's followers by opening fire with sub-machine guns. In the subsequent election, as the army "guarded" the ballot boxes, Trujillo was elected President "without opposition."

Thousands of personal and political enemies were quickly eliminated by execution. When bodies piled up faster than his troops could dispose of them, a hurricane relieved Trujillo's embarrassment. Claiming it had killed twenty-five hundred Dominicans, he had the bodies piled in the city square, drenched with gasoline and set afire. "This speedy action," he lied, "has saved our country from a horrible plague."

Rafael Trujillo. (*Photograph by Enriquillo Durdáçn*)

Trujillo lost no time in extorting money for himself and his family, a fortune that eventually grew to thirty million dollars a year. Raising the price of salt from two cents to twelve cents a pound allowed him to bank four hundred thousand dollars annually. He pocketed unrecorded "taxes" received from every business. To hold a Dominican government job, employees had to "donate" ten per cent of their pay to his Dominican Party. Soldiers had to pay half their fifteen dollars monthly salary for laundry to a monopoly owned by one of Trujillo's mistresses.

His son Ramfis was made an army colonel at the age of three, with full pay and privileges, but had to wait until his tenth birthday to become a brigadier general! Relatives were put in charge of every monopoly Trujillo did not control himself. The distinction between family holdings and government finances became so blurred that once he paid a huge Dominican debt with a personal check. A later estimate of the fortune he salted away as dictator was put at eight hundred million dollars.

Propagandists who hailed him as a "highly efficient administrator" neglected to add that his efficiency merely lined his own pockets. They told how he provided "free" milk when milk prices soared. But not that he had forced dairies to sell it to him at three cents a bottle; that he had sold it to his Dominican Party for five cents a bottle; and that only *then* was it distributed.

Promoting himself to Generalissimo, Trujillo also became Founder and Supreme Chief, Savior of the Republic, Benefactor of the Fatherland, and Restorer of Finances. Public buildings and two thousand statues of him went up to glorify his reign. A giant neon sign on one building flashed the motto: GOD AND TRUJILLO. His captive press often referred to it in more respectful terms: TRUJILLO AND GOD.

"He is the hymn of glory," wrote one editor, "that falls among us as a rain of fragrant petals, as the wings of white butterflies." Small wonder that, when he visited his old home, he reproached his aging father petulantly, "Father, rise to your feet when the President of the Republic arrives!"

Trusting no one, he made every appointee to office sign and give him an undated resignation. He controlled those around him through fear or bribery. Anyone he considered too intelligent was either bought off or killed and his body dumped into shark-infested waters. Once, made suspicious by hearing cheers for a crony, he ordered that person, a colonel, jailed in irons. The prisoner spat in the dictator's face. "Yes, Trujillo," he cried, "I am a murderer—but with courage. You are a murderer—but a coward!" Next day he was "found" hanging in his cell.

Steel whips awaited any Dominican rash enough to protest any act of Trujillo's. "I was alone in a cell just a little over two feet wide and not quite six feet in length," one victim revealed. "I couldn't see out and there was scarcely any air. I lay there for days in terrible pain, with only a little bread and a small quantity of water. They would take me out and repeat the beatings every so often."

In 1933 a revolution in Cuba sent its dictator, Gerardo Machado, fleeing to Trujillo's island for refuge. "Rafael, learn from my misfortune," he sighed. "Whatever you do, avoid bad publicity in the American press. You are only safe so long as the Yankees support you!" Trujillo quickly passed a law making it a criminal offense to speak or write against him.

Weeks later an eighteen-year-old Puerto Rican youth who "spoke disrespectfully" of him was arrested and shot. Trujillo grew nervous when Washington learned of it and demanded he explain such treatment of an American citizen. He blamed the "stupidity" of an army lieutenant, who was promptly arrested and "shot while trying to escape."

In return for the high taxes he extorted, Trujillo permitted over two hundred thousand Haitian Negroes to live in the Dominican Republic as labor for American-owned sugar plantations. But in 1937, with a crash in the price of sugar, many thousands were laid off. Some stole food to live. Trujillo pondered the problem. "Dominicans would be happier," he told his army commander, "if we got rid of the Haitians."

Over twelve thousand of them were slaughtered in cold blood, many cut to pieces with machetes. Their bodies were trucked to ravines and dumped, or piled onto fishing boats and thrown to the sharks. So that news of the slaughter would not leak out, Trujillo clamped tight censorship on all mail and news dispatches.

A shocked American missionary, Father Barnes, wrote about the massacre in a letter to his sister. It never reached her. He was found on the floor of his home, murdered brutally. But the news leaked out, stirring a decision by the United States, Mexico, and Cuba to make a joint investigation.

Alarmed, Trujillo rushed notes to all three powers protesting, "A few Haitians were killed by Dominican farmers provoked by the loss of cattle and produce to thieving Haitians. We have arrested ten of the farmers involved in this regrettable incident." Paying President Vincent of Haiti a seven-hundred-fifty-thousand-dollar indemnity, he placed full page ads in American papers assuring everyone that an investigation was unnecessary because he had settled the matter amicably with Haiti.

But General Hugh Johnson, a former New Deal official, shocked Americans by a broadcast describing how Haitian women had been stabbed and mutilated, babies bayoneted, and men tied up and thrown into the sea to drown. Congressman Hamilton Fish, ranking member of the House Foreign Affairs Committee, shouted in Congress, "This is the most outrageous atrocity that has ever been perpetrated in the American hemisphere!" He demanded a break in relations with Trujillo.

Hoping to cool the uproar, the worried dictator announced he would not run for "re-election" in 1938. A figurehead was put in the President's chair while he continued to run the country with an iron hand. Anxious about his image in the United

States, he determined to whitewash it at all costs. A defector later revealed to the *New York Times* that Trujillo had spent five million dollars on "some U.S. Congressmen and State Department officials," and another five million dollars on lobbyists and press agents to "take care of" the press and public for him.

His press agents advised him to offer asylum to Loyalist refugees from Spain and Jewish refugees from Germany, so that they could publicize him as a humanitarian. His brother objected that refugees were dangerous—they hated dictators. "Our spies will keep an eye on them," Trujillo said. "I need the publicity. Besides, intelligent immigrants with healthy white blood will improve our line!"

His American publicity machine began churning out books and articles praising him as a great statesman; one article even recommended him for the Nobel Peace Prize. But when President Franklin Roosevelt invited Latin-American leaders to visit the White House, Trujillo was pointedly ignored. He went to the United States anyhow, buying a private yacht for the trip.

His paid agents arranged an official reception for him, with Marine guard and band, in Miami. Principal speaker at a dinner for him in New York was none other than Congressman Hamilton Fish, who had denounced him in Congress. Later when it was found that twenty-five thousand dollars had been deposited to his bank account by Trujillo, he explained that it was a business transaction. Outside the hotel pickets carried signs: "We object to the visit of the bloodiest dictator the world has ever known!"

By 1942 Trujillo felt secure enough to take back the presidency of the Dominican Republic. He allowed two political parties to campaign. The candidate of one party was Rafael Trujillo. The candidate of the other was also Rafael Trujillo. Trujillo won.

He continued wooing influential Americans. To ensure large United States purchases of Dominican sugar at high prices, he left the sugar industry largely in the hands of American interests.

His "sugar tax" brought him a half million dollars annually, more than his series of wives and mistresses needed to maintain his five elaborate houses.

He entertained United States government and business officials and their families in the grand style of a Roman emperor. Guests who were given three-month free vacations in the Dominican Republic returned home full of praise. The chairman of the Senate Agriculture Committee described Trujillo as "the sort of leader we need more of in Latin America."

His press agents persistently sold him to Americans as a "defender of the Western Hemisphere against the Communist menace." When he permitted the United States to install a guided-missile tracking base, the American ambassador praised him highly, assuring the Dominican people, "No one can gainsay the great benefits he has already succeeded in bringing about." Those receiving the starvation wages of less than twenty cents a day, may not have agreed.

Trujillo's political enemies who had fled into exile, and worked for his overthrow overseas, lived in constant danger of their lives. His professional killers murdered one Dominican editor in a New York hallway in 1952. Dr. Jesus Maria de Galindez, an anti-Trujillo professor teaching at Columbia University, was kidnapped in 1956. Drugged and flown to the Dominican Republic, seems that Galindez was boiled to death.

When *Life, Time* and the Columbia Broadcasting System (CBS) broke the story, Trujillo spent another half million dollars through his press agents to label the Galindez case a Red plot to discredit him. Not only did this crude ruse fail, but his son Ramfis attracted more unflattering headlines by flying polo ponies to Paris and showering Hollywood actresses with fur coats and sports cars. Was this, asked the press, how United States aid money was spent?

By 1960 opposition to the Trujillo regime was spreading rapidly both at home and abroad. Alarmed, he bought fifty million dollars' worth of military equipment in Europe, and drafted an additional six thousand men into his army. Arresting a thousand Dominicans he suspected of disloyalty, he accused the Catholic Church of being the chief conspirator against him.

"This kind of attack," snapped President Eisenhower in disgust, "is usually the last desperate resort of a dictator." He tried to block an increase in the Dominican sugar quota that Trujillo's paid lobbyists had won for him in Congress. The Organization of American States (OAS) now took its cue from Washington. Led by President Rómulo Betancourt of Venezuela, the OAS accused Trujillo of "flagrant and widespread violation of human rights."

Enraged, he plotted the overthrow of the Venezuelan government and the assassination of Betancourt. Both attempts failed. The OAS urged all Latin American nations to break off relations with the Dominican Republic. In a desperate attempt to save himself, Trujillo tried to get the support of Cuba and Russia— the Communist nations he purported to hate.

Eight disgusted Dominican generals, led by Brigadier General Antonio Imbert Barrera, decided that they had had enough. On May 30, 1961, Trujillo's thirty-one-year dictatorship came to a violent end as he fell victim to their bullets. Turmoil swept the Dominican Republic as contending groups struggled for power.

A new United States ambassador to Santo Domingo grimly reported his findings to Washington: "There is nothing here to build on . . . no government, no labor unions, no free civic associations . . . no money, no work, no going economy, no civil service, no democratic traditions, nothing."

This was the glorious heritage left by the dictator who had once been publicly eulogized by the ranking member of the House Foreign Affairs Committee in these words:

"General, you have created a golden age for your country, and I am proud and happy to repeat at this time to a United States audience that you will go down in the history of your country as a builder greater than all the Spanish Conquistadors together!"

7

Cuba

I. Fulgencio Batista (1901–1973)

Batista grew up barefoot, hungry, and ignorant in an Oriente Province village controlled by the United Fruit Company, whose officials lived in a comfort he envied. He worshiped an older brother who died of tuberculosis because of lack of any treatment facilities for Cuba's peasantry.

An ambitious youth, Batista worked as a tailor's assistant, sugarcane cutter, grocery clerk, apprentice barber, and railway brakeman before deciding that he needed an education to get ahead. At twenty-one he joined the army to attend its night school. Becoming a court stenographer at army courts-martial, he grew aware of the extent of opposition to the dictatorship of Gerardo Machado, the corrupt politician who had seized power in 1924. He developed close ties with other enlisted men at the bases all over Cuba where his work took him.

After twelve years as a private, he was promoted to sergeant. By this time he had become the central figure in a web of revolutionary cells. In 1933, sparked by labor unrest in the United States, Cuba's workers dared to defy Machado by calling a general strike. Batista decided that his hour of destiny had struck. He gave the signal for a sergeants' revolt. At every military post, early in the morning while the officers slept, key sergeants took over command of the entire Cuban army.

An elated Batista promptly promoted himself to colonel and chief of the army. Dismissing every Machado officer, he replaced them from the ranks. He wired one sergeant: EFFECTIVE IMMEDIATELY YOU ARE PROMOTED TO CAPTAIN. ACKNOWLEDGE. Back came the answer: YOUR WIRE TOO LATE. I ALREADY PROMOTED MYSELF TO COLONEL. Amused, Batista consented.

For the next seven years he ran Cuba from behind a screen of puppet presidents. Whenever one of them refused to take his orders, Batista simply "lifted his finger" and the Cuban legislature impeached the offender. Entrenching himself in power, he used police and troops to shut down opposition newspapers, imprison and torture editors, and frighten rival politicians into exile in Miami.

He married twice and fathered five children, doting on his first son, whom he dressed in a sergeant's uniform and called "the little sergeant." He boasted, "I don't know who my father was, but *my* son can say, 'My papa is Batista!' "

Like most dictators, he yearned for a patina of respectability. In 1938 he won an invitation to Washington from General Malin Craig, United States Chief of Staff. Worrying about the six rows of gaudy medals he had awarded to himself, he asked how many rows of decorations General Craig wore.

"One," said his orderly. Batista fumed, *"Nombre de Dios!* I will not go to Washington looking like a monkey on a stick. Rip off all my medals . . . except the top *two* rows!"

He never lost his thirst for the education denied him as a peasant child. Teaching himself English when he was almost forty, he began reading Karl Marx, Plato, Darwin, and Spengler.

Marx opened his eyes to the need for government programs to help the poor. Plato taught him how to be persuasive in argument. Darwin made him cynical about church teachings, except insofar as he could use them to discourage revolt. Spengler made him wary of Communists and socialists.

At this period Cubans saw him as a good-natured, friendly man, powerfully built with straight dark hair and somewhat oriental eyes. Despite his ruthlessness as a dictator, they felt that he was still one of them—a poor boy who hated the privileged rich and wanted to help the masses.

Batista decided to risk taking off his uniform to run for office as President. "Now," he told the Cuban people, "I can truthfully say that I am one of you." He won handsomely in an honest election. Even the Communist Party supported him, and he rewarded them with a small voice in his new government. "They are far less dangerous in a coalition government with me where I can control them," he said privately, "than kept out to organize a revolution!"

Army chiefs who had been part of the sergeants' conspiracy were not convinced, and threatened to revolt. Batista spent a whole night from sunset to sunrise coaxing their support. One hour after they reluctantly agreed, they were arrested, hustled aboard a ship, and headed for exile in Miami. Batista warned other army officers never to interfere in the new civilian era dawning for Cuba.

In his new role as President he launched health, education, and public works programs. In memory of the older brother he mourned, he built a million-dollar tuberculosis sanitarium. A beautiful children's playground went up in Havana. He built hundreds of schools, passed laws to protect workers, divided big sugar estates into small farms for the poor, built roads and highways.

Although his programs were popular, Batista himself was not. The Cuban people knew that he was taking graft. Half the profits of gambling casinos were paid to his wife. At the first opportunity they defeated him at the polls and forced him to retire to Florida, consoled by a personal fortune of forty million dollars. However, after four years of bored idleness, he received permission to return to Havana in 1948. He ran for a Senate seat and won.

In 1952 he once more sought the presidency, but was cha-grined when it became clear that he was running a poor third in the race. He began conspiring with young army officers. Two months before election day he put on his old general's uniform and led a bloodless army coup to throw out President Carlos Prío Socarrás, assuming dictatorial powers as "Chief of State."

A young lawyer by the name of Fidel Castro who had been running as a candidate for Congress from Havana swore to die if necessary to destroy the usurper who had crushed Cuban democracy. Then he fled to Oriente Province to raise a rebel army.

As greedy for graft as ever, Batista made a deal with American gangsters. They received gambling and vice privileges in Havana in return for a fat cut of profits derived from a rich and growing tourist trade. Worried by Castro's rapidly growing army of guer-rillas, Batista suspended all civil rights. A "Law of Public Order" forbade the press to criticize the government. He was jubilant when Castro was captured and put on trial.

"Condemn me!" the rebel cried defiantly in court. "It doesn't matter. History will absolve me!" He was sentenced to a fifteen-year jail term, unshakably convinced of Victor Hugo's dictum: "When dictatorship is a fact, revolution becomes a right."

Batista grew worried when he appeared in public and crowds cheered for Castro, rather than for him.

He granted amnesty to political prisoners so that Castro and his followers would leave the country while he rigged an election to get himself legally made President. But in six months Castro returned to the mountains of Oriente Province to organize a new revolution. The island rumbled with growing discontent over Batista's rule.

Businessmen were fed up with his graft-ridden wheeling and dealing. Peasants were angered by his failure to keep his promise of widespread land reforms. Intellectuals deplored his habit of scrapping any law that displeased him. Workers hated his brutal troops. Soldiers resented their low pay, well aware of the millions he stole from the treasury.

Sensing the coming storm, Washington withdrew its Cuban ambassador, Arthur Gardner, who had become too closely identified with Batista's tyranny. "Mr. Gardner behaved more like a businessman than an ambassador," observed one Havana editor, "and made notorious mistakes." The new ambassador, Earl Smith, was greeted in Havana by women demonstrators who urged him to help restore Cuban freedom.

As opposition to Batista's regime mounted, he resorted to terror to crush it. Filling the jails with his opponents, he had them whipped, their faces scarred, their ribs and bones broken. Over twenty thousand Cubans were executed, many bulldozed into common graves, others hung up as a grim warning.

Batista played on Washington's fears of a Castro revolution by demanding proof of United States support that he could have published in the Cuban press. One American major general flew into Havana to decorate a Batista general with the Legion of Merit. Another such general publicly praised Batista as a great Latin American leader. Secretary of State John Foster Dulles attended a Cuban embassy dinner in Washington and toasted Batista.

Finally in March 1958 President Eisenhower stopped arms shipments to Batista. "Obviously Castro had won the emotional support of the Cuban people," he explained later. There were wholesale desertions from government forces to Castro's guerrilla army.

In desperation, Batista flooded Oriente Province with posters offering a hundred thousand dollars for the head of his enemy. Ten civilians in Castro territory were ordered executed for every government soldier killed. When Batista demanded the bombing of all cities held by Castro, most of his air force quit in disgust and went over to the rebels.

As doom closed in around him, Batista prudently cached abroad a personal fortune estimated at over two hundred million dollars.

Castro's rebels speared toward Havana, joined by jubilant peasants. Batista's generals suddenly confronted him with a demand for his resignation. In the chill early morning hours of New Year's Day, 1959, he fled for his life, seeking asylum in the Dominican Republic. When Trujillo fell two years later, Batista left for Portugal, where he lived the rest of his life in comfort and obscurity.

So ended the rule of a dictator Plato might have been describing in *The Republic* over two thousand years ago: "When he first appears above ground he is a protector. . . . At first in the early days of his power he is full of smiles, and he salutes everyone whom he meets—he to be called a tyrant, who is making promises in public and also in private . . . wanting to be so kind and good to everyone!" Then he keeps the people "impoverished by payment of taxes . . . compelled to devote themselves to their daily wants and therefore less likely to conspire against him."

But for every Batista, a grim Castro lies waiting.

II. Fidel Castro (1926-)

One of Castro's first ministers said of him, "He speaks until he is tired. He eats until he is satisfied. He moves until he is exhausted. He will fight until he is killed. He rebelled against Batista, against the Cuban community, against the United States. He will rebel against Russia . . . in his permanent rebellion." What strange discontent drives him?

Fidel's father was a rich Oriente Province landowner whose shady deals financed two marriages and seven children in considerable comfort. It was a quarrelsome household, however. Fidel Castro grew up alienated from his family, except for a younger brother Raúl and sister Juanita.

Given a Catholic education in Santiago and Havana, he distinguished himself as both scholar and athlete, excelling in basketball, baseball, and track. "He has known how to win the admiration and the affection of all," observed his high school yearbook. At the University of Havana Law School he demonstrated a strong urge for outdoor adventure.

Becoming head of an explorers' club, he once led a hike in the Sierra de los Órganos when cloudbursts flooded a valley they had to cross. Castro jumped into the boiling rapids with one end of a rope clenched between his teeth, fighting his way to the other bank. Then he anchored the rope to a tree and helped pull the others through the dangerous currents.

During his mountain trips, he came across Dominican exiles training in secret to overthrow Trujillo. His love of adventure, plus an intellectual hatred for dictators, led him to join their expedition in August 1947. Their invasion fleet was intercepted and attacked. Castro escaped by diving overboard and swimming ashore with his tommy gun.

Back at the university he became head of the law school's student government body. In October, he married a fellow student, Mirtha Díaz Balart, who later divorced him after they had had a son. His idealism was fired by Eduardo Chibás, a reformer demanding honest government on behalf of Cuba's poor. Upon graduating in 1950, Castro spent most of his time defending penniless Cubans who could not afford lawyers.

Two years later, when Batista overthrew President Prío Socarrás, Castro dared to file charges against him in a Havana court, demanding a hundred-year prison term for the dictator. Forced to flee to the mountains of Oriente, he gathered a following of 170 young rebels and led them in a desperate attack on a Santiago army barracks, hoping to spark a general uprising.

"We give the first cry of liberty or death!" he shouted.

It was death for most. Castro was captured and put on trial. Acting as his own lawyer, he turned the courtroom into a political forum. "Every military fort should be turned into a school, and instead of soldiers should house ten thousand orphan children!" he declared. "The United Fruit Company owns land

Fulgencio Batista. (*U. S. Office of War Information*)

Fidel Castro. (*United Nations*)

from the north to the south coast in Oriente Province—but two hundred thousand Cuban families there don't own an inch of land!"

After a time in jail, his amnesty and exile in Mexico gave him the opportunity to build the 26th of July Movement—named after the date of his first unsuccessful revolt. His brother Raul and Che Guevara, a Leftist, helped him raise funds in Florida and New York to mount a new revolution.

"I handled nearly twenty thousand pesos," Castro recalled later. "Yet how many times were we lacking milk for my son! How many times did the hard-hearted electric company cut off my electricity! I still keep the miserable court papers by which the landowners dispossess tenants. I had no personal income, but practically lived on the charity of my friends. I know what it is to see a son suffering from hunger while having, in my pockets, money belonging to the cause."

When Mexican police raided his headquarters, they found a hidden arsenal. Castro was coldly warned that if he and his men did not leave Mexico they would be deported to Cuba.

"Wonderful!" he grinned. "That's where we want to go!"

In December 1956, he and eighty-two followers sailed for the eastern tip of Cuba in a battered old yacht. Batista was expecting them: Castro had boldly announced his invasion in advance. "I want everyone in Cuba to know that I am coming," he insisted. "It is psychological warfare!"

The Cuban Air Force spotted their landing and flew over them bombing and strafing. They were forced to hide in canefields for a week, surviving on sugar cane. Most of the rebels were flushed out and captured. Castro himself, Raúl Castro, Guevara, and a dozen survivors fled into the foothills of the Sierra Maestra. "Don't worry," Fidel told them confidently, "The days of the dictatorship are numbered!" A few thought him mad.

Growing beards to avoid the nuisance of shaving, they became known as the *barbudos*—the bearded ones. Castro led them on raids against rich landowners, who were "tried" in a kangaroo court and executed. Their lands were turned over to poor peasants, who were understandably enthusiastic about the Robin Hood of the Sierra Maestra. They supported "Fidelismo" with food and volunteers. Although the Church took a dim view of his violence and agnosticism, some clergy upheld him.

"Fidel Castro is a man of destiny," declared Father Armando Llorente of the Colegio de Belén. "Behind him is the hand of God. He has a mission to fulfill and he will fulfill it against all obstacles. Fidel is going to do a lot of good for the poor people and the humble. His special friends at school were always the porters, cooks, and workmen."

Batista branded Castro a Communist and tool of Moscow. But the rebel leader had rebuffed the Cuban Communist Party's attempt to join him in a united front against Batista.

"I never have been nor am I a Communist," he insisted. "If I were, I would have sufficient courage to proclaim it!"

In order to bring down the Batista regime, he decided that it must be cut off from its chief source of wealth—the cane crop. He began burning the sugarcane fields. One of the first he ordered set afire was his own family's plantation. His two-year struggle against Batista brought him a good deal of sympathy from the American press and public, if not from official Washington. Herbert Matthews of the *New York Times* saw him as "the most remarkable and romantic figure to arise in Cuban history." Acknowledging Castro's tremendous popularity when he came to power in January 1959, after Batista's flight, the United States recognized his regime six days later.

Embraced everywhere by wildly enthusiastic crowds, Castro made a triumphant tour of Cuba in a captured helicopter. "I won't exchange it for anything or anybody!" he said enthusiastically. "It's mine now—all mine!" It was the only booty the thirty-two-year-old conqueror of Cuba claimed for himself. For the first time Cuba had a genuine hero uncorrupted by greed for riches or luxury. This novelty also captured the imagination of the Latin-American masses everywhere.

But even if Fidel Castro was personally honest, he quickly proved to be no more of a democrat than the dictator he had overthrown. He had accused Batista of betraying Cuba's Constitution of 1940, but he himself replaced it with a new "Fundamental Law" that gave him personal power to expropriate private property, settle labor disputes, and spend funds.

He court-martialed Batista officers and airmen for "crimes against the people." Condemned by revolutionary tribunals, over five hundred were sent before the firing squad. The attorney for one defendant asked that charges be dismissed for lack of proof. "He has to be shot anyway," the prosecutor said, "as a measure of social health."

Castro was baffled by the shocked outcries his bloodbath provoked in North and South America. "Batista never even gave anyone a fair trial," he said indignantly. "He just had them killed and no one protested. These men are *assassins,* not just innocent people or political opponents. We are executing murderers who deserve to be shot. If I had let our forces kill them in the last days of fighting, nothing would have been said. There are protests only because I gave them a trial and a chance to see a priest before execution!"

He lashed out at Washington for having supplied Batista with the tanks, guns, planes, and bombs that had killed thousands of Cubans, and for "fifty years of interference in Cuban affairs." He threatened, "If there should again be intervention in Cuba, two hundred thousand gringos will be killed!"

Sharply cutting back the regular army, he turned one major army post into a school. "The last thing I am is a military man," he vowed. "I have no medals. I don't like armaments. Ours is now a country without generals and colonels!" He refused to promote himself from his rebel rank of major.

He began his reform program by slashing rents in half. Confiscating thirteen per cent of Cuba's farmland, he divided it into cooperative farms, and did not spare some of his own family's estates. His brother Ramón furiously blamed Raúl Castro: "Raúl is a dirty little Communist. Someday I am going to kill him!" The Cuban Communist Party supported Fidel enthusiastically, and members were now given some key appointments.

Castro worked around the clock with inexhaustible energy to transform the Cuban economy. Warned he would collapse unless he rested, he laughed. "My medicine is the people," he said. "I thrive on seeing and talking to the people!"

He resisted all demands that he hold elections, explaining seriously, "They would be unfair because I would be swept into office." He was undoubtedly a hero to the Cuban masses, but the island's middle class preferred exile in Miami, Florida, to life under his revolutionary regime. They were incensed when he took over Catholic schools, banned religious processions, and arrested priests who protested. He jailed over forty Baptist ministers as "Bible-packing CIA agents." His own mother bitterly protested his rabid anti-clericalism.

In April 1959, despite a distinct coolness toward him in Washington, he decided to visit the United States to try for a Cuban-American accord. President Eisenhower snubbed him by flying off to Georgia to play golf, turning him over to Vice President Nixon, who, Castro later said ruefully, "spent the whole time scolding me." Democrats were annoyed.

Senator John F. Kennedy attacked the Eisenhower Administration for failing to give "the fiery young rebel a warmer welcome in his hour of triumph." Former President Harry Truman declared, "I think that Fidel Castro is a good young man who has made mistakes, but who seems to want to do the right thing for the Cuban people, and we ought to . . . help him."

Rebuffed by Washington, Castro turned to the Communist world, which quickly talked business. He received a hundred-million-dollar loan, orders for a million tons of Cuban sugar annually, and a promise of army planes. Moving to the Left, he began confiscating American-owned business property in Cuba.

What worried Washington even more was his open encouragement of revolution in other Latin American countries. President Eisenhower angrily slashed United States imports of Cuban sugar, and let the Central Intelligence Agency (CIA) proceed with a secret plot to overthrow the Cuban government. On January 3, 1961, an insolent demand by Castro led Eisenhower to sever diplomatic relations, and to stop Americans from traveling to Cuba.

In the United Nations Security Council, Castro charged the United States with planning an armed invasion of Cuba. Washington denied it, but *The Nation* and the *St. Louis Post-Dispatch* confirmed that the CIA was training a Cuban invasion force in Guatemala.

When Kennedy replaced Eisenhower as president, his advisers strongly urged him to go through with the plan, assuring him the invasion would touch off a great Cuban uprising against Castro. Kennedy hesitantly gave the signal for the Bay of Pigs invasion on April 17, 1961. It was a dismal fiasco. Many of the invaders were killed and 1,100 taken prisoner. Castro later traded them to the United States for badly needed supplies.

American prestige suffered a black eye. Castro had been proved right in his charges that the United States was intervening in Latin America to overthrow him. The Cuban people were incensed at what they considered another flagrant act of old-style American imperialism. America's own allies were sharply critical. Furious at the advisers who had misled him, Kennedy groaned, "How could I have agreed to such a stupid mistake!" But publicly he took full blame for the fiasco.

On May Day, 1961, Castro angrily declared Cuba a socialist country. "If Mr. Kennedy does not like socialism," he cried, "we don't like imperialism, we don't like capitalism!" At the end of the year he announced that there would be no more elections in Cuba. "I am a Marxist-Leninist," he finally declared defiantly, "and will be to the day I die!"

Until the Bay of Pigs blunder, Castro's popularity had been faltering because of his failure to solve Cuba's economic problems. But now the Latin American masses saw him as a Caribbean David defying the North American Goliath. His picture occupied a place of honor in the shacks of Honduran banana peasants, Costa Rican coffee hands, Venezuelan oil workers, Chilean miners. His Marxism meant nothing to them; his victory over *"imperialismo yanqui"* everything.

In 1962 Castro inspired one hundred thousand teenage volunteers to fan out through Cuba on a double mission—to end peasant illiteracy at the same time they helped bring in the cane crop. They were thrilled to see Castro himself, barechested in a peasant straw hat, chopping cane with them on weekends. Hands were short because thousands of peasants preferred to work on their own small holdings. Castro now regretted having divided up the big farms instead of making them collectives.

A food shortage compelled him to cut the Cuban rice ration in half. "Conditions in Cuba will surely get better," he promised, "in the next ten or twelve years." But in the port city of Cárdenas, embittered crowds surged through the streets shouting, "We are hungry! Down with Communism!" He sent Russian T-34 tanks through Cárdenas to disperse what his puppet President, Osvaldo Dorticós, denounced as a "wretched counterrevolutionary provocation."

In October Castro permitted five thousand Russian technicians secretly to install ballistic missiles on Cuban soil. If Washington tried another Bay of Pigs, he vowed, the Yankees would pay for it. When Kennedy learned what was going on, he threw a naval blockade around Cuba and forced Khrushchev to dismantle and take home the missiles. Despite the setback, Castro could not help feeling a sense of great power: for a few hours he had brought the whole world to the brink of nuclear war.

His prestige plunged severely in 1964, however, when the press learned that his sister Juanita had fled to Mexico, and admitted she had been helping Cuban refugees escape. "I cannot longer remain indifferent to what is happening in my country," she declared. "My brothers Fidel and Raúl have made it an enormous prison surrounded by water. The people are nailed to a cross of torment imposed by international Communism." Accusing the United States Embassy in Mexico City of having written her statement, Fidel nevertheless admitted sadly, "This incident for me is personally very bitter."

When President Johnson succeeded Kennedy after his assassination in Dallas, Castro sought a new understanding with Washington. "We will no longer give aid to revolutionary movements in other Latin American countries," he promised, "if you will end your own subversive activity inside Cuba. We do not hate you. If the United States is ready to live with us, then we would feel the same obligation."

President Johnson maintained a steely silence.

In a marathon speech in 1965, Castro told Cubans, "Imagine that one day there would be a total blockade through which no fuel, nothing could pass. A man from the Sierra Maestra would merely say that he had lived his life without fuel, without electricity, without transport, without medicine, without anything at all." He added defiantly, "Today the people can cut cane with one hand, and crush any invasion of mercenaries with the other!"

But his bravado could not disguise the fact that Cuba's economy was in bad shape because of the flight of its educated professionals and executives among the two hundred thousand middle- and upper-class Cubans going to the United States. Bungling had caused a chronic shortage of all consumer goods.

"We are ashamed," Castro admitted. "Who is to blame? The administrators, the rulers, everyone!" Everything his inept administration touched seemed to fall to pieces. Soon after the Hilton Hotel in Havana was taken over by the government, the doors didn't work, the bellboys wore dirty uniforms, the lobby roof leaked, half the elevators didn't run.

By 1967, rural income was an annual ninety dollars per capita. Only one family in ten had milk to drink; only one in twenty-five ate meat. Over a third of the Cubans were jobless; forty-three per cent still illiterate; thirty-six per cent suffering from intestinal parasites. Yet Father Felipe de la Cruz, a parish priest of San Jose who sharply criticized Castro's anti-religious measures, still confessed that he approved of the revolution because Castro had done more for the health and education of Cuba's poor masses than had any ruler before him.

Despite the setbacks, by 1970 Fidel had completed the nationalization of the Cuban economy. All trade and manufacturing as well as the majority of agricultural land were under the control of the state. Economic activity was centrally organized with resources allocated according to a state-run plan.

The culmination of this movement was Castro's decision to concentrate the country's resources in order to produce 10 million tons of sugar in 1970. The massive undertaking involved a coordinated effort from all sectors of Cuba's economy. The primary goal of the plan was to use funds from the sugar's export to finance industrialization, but as with many of Castro's state run directives, the final harvest fell short of the goal, producing only 8.5 million tons.

Due to the prominence of the plan, the failure was a significant blow to the prestige of the revolution. Surprisingly, Castro took full responsibility. The failure led him to acknowledge that he could not achieve quick economic independence from the Soviet Union, so in 1972 Cuba became a member of the Soviet Union's economic association, the Council for Mutual Economic Assistance (CMEA).

Meanwhile, Castro had established himself as an international leader in the revolutionary movement. He saw revolution in Latin America as inevitable due to class and economic exploitation, and he openly offered support to revolutionary causes around the world. With help from the Soviet Union, Castro gave military support to revolutionary movements in Nicaragua, Guatemala, Venezuela, Colombia, and later in Angola and Ethiopia.

The arrival of the 1970s saw Castro pursue a more moderate approach to foreign affairs and domestic policy. Changes were made gradually, and Cuba aligned itself closer with the Soviet Union, which resulted in favorable trade relations. While standards of living were not overly high, Cuba did, during this time period, create an egalitarian society, largely free of the malnutrition that characterized many of its Caribbean neighbors.

However, the collapse of the Soviet Union in 1991 meant the end of significant trade relations and subsidies. It was a massive blow to the Cuban economy, as nearly 90 per cent of its foreign trade came from the Soviet Union and members of the CMEA. Overnight, shortages racked the Cuban economy, which ground to a halt. The economic free fall fed social unrest that led in 1994 to open anti-government demonstrations in Cuba for the first time since 1959. That summer, Castro opened up his ports, allowing thousands of unhappy Cubans to go to the U.S.

In dealing with the economic crises, Castro showed considerable flexibility. He introduced certain free-market principles into Cuba's economy by licensing some small businesses and opening private agricultural markets, allowing producers to sell directly to the consumer. He also encouraged foreign investment, especially in Cuba's tourism industry. As a result, the expected implosion of Cuba's economy after the collapse of the Soviet Union never occurred.

Starting in 2006, Castro began to slowly relinquish control. On July 31st of that year, he provisionally passed power to his brother, Raúl, as he recovered from surgery. Then in 2008, he announced that he would not accept another term as president. Finally, in 2011, he stepped down as secretary-general of the Communist Party of Cuba where he was once again succeeded by Raúl.

Castro's legacy remains a complicated one. Despite forty years of unrelenting pressure from the United States, Castro and his communist party have remained in power. Throughout much of Castro's reign, the daily lives of the average Cuban revolved around obtaining basic necessities. Long lines for rationed food and inconsistent public transportation were facts of life. Yet, despite his country's many crises, Castro never lost sight of his socialist principles. The sacrifice for economic hardships were shared by all, and the free medical and educational systems were maintained.

HAITI
François Duvalier (1907–1971)

White-haired, dark-skinned, his eyes cunning behind thick glasses, he sat beside a delicate white phone in a gingerbread palace in Port-au-Prince. Keys to the armory and treasury hung from a string around his neck. He suspected everyone of plotting to destroy him, and kept a loaded Colt .45 on his desk beside a Bible open at the Book of Psalms.

In 1966 he broke his brooding isolation to talk to an American reporter who asked him the purpose of the gun. "Papa Doc" Duvalier picked it up and stared at it as though he had never seen it before. "That's a mistake," he said, handing it to an aide. "Take it away!"

During Duvalier's reign, two army units of eight hundred men stood guard day and night outside his palace. The city remained deathly quiet except for patrols of his private army

François Duvalier (*Wide World Photos*)

and a few French-speaking Negro peasants carrying baskets of food to a street market. An air of decay, fear, and oppression hung over Port-au-Prince, the capital of Haiti.

Posters glorifying Papa Doc could be found everywhere. One showed Jesus with his arm around the dictator, telling Haitians, "I have chosen him." At night neon signs flashed his proverbs to the people: "I am the flag, one and indivisible." . . . "I have no enemies but the enemies of Haiti."

In Port-au-Prince, one learned to guard opinions. Cables were censored, phone conversations monitored, foreigners' homes staffed with servant-spies. One diplomat revealed that each of his three servants informed on the others.

Most of Haiti's 4,700,000 people suffered from serious malnutrition, their small rocky farm plots producing a meagre diet of rice, corn, beans, and mangoes. Annual per capita income was the lowest in the hemisphere—seventy dollars a year, according to Duvalier; fifteen dollars a year, according to his enemies.

Peasants streamed into Port-au-Prince looking for nonexistent jobs, sleeping in the smelly, dusty streets, begging a few coins to stay alive. Many of Haiti's coffee plantations had been wrecked by hurricanes and mismanagement. Some thirty thousand Haitians crossed the border every day to work on Dominican sugar plantations. Most of Papa Doc's peasants were so poor that to go to town a man had to borrow clothes from five or six friends or else go in rags.

Yet they were too crushed and illiterate to blame Duvalier for their miserable lives. He was held in superstitious awe as chief practitioner of Haitian voodoo, the religion of witchcraft imported by African slaves. His photo adorned voodoo shrines, and widespread tales were whispered about the ghoulish rites he performed with dead enemies.

Once Papa Doc decided that he needed a model city to attract tourists. Extorting money from Haitian businessmen, he began building Duvalierville twenty miles out of the capital. Then he suddenly lost interest. His model city was abandoned, consisting of only a few unfinished houses, an empty supermarket, a vacant bank without a door, a movie theater that had never shown a film, a restaurant that had never served a meal.

The rest of Haiti was equally desolate. Impassable roads disappeared completely in the rainy season. The eye searched in vain for schools, bridges, public buildings. Phones seldom operated. Electricity disappeared at nightfall.

Unlike Communist or even Fascist dictators, Duvalier saw no need to beguile his subjects with bread and circuses, or even promises of a better life. He considered it enough to keep them in the abject state of hopeless despair that has characterized most of Haitian history.

In 1697, the island was wrested from Spanish colonists by French pirates, who brought in African slaves to work the plantations. Mistreated, starved, plagued by hurricanes and tropical disease, they finally revolted in 1801. Their leader, Toussaint L'Ouverture, seized power, but was soon overthrown by Napoléon's troops. A Haitian general named Dessalines threw the French out in 1804 and proclaimed himself Emperor. His two-year rule as a despot ended with his assassination.

Haiti has been in turmoil ever since, with mulattoes (seven per cent of the population) struggling with Negroes (ninety-three per cent) for supremacy. The better educated mulattoes have usually dominated the island's political and economic life, working with American interests which owned sugar and sisal plantations, power companies, copper and bauxite mines, meat-packing and oil companies in Haiti.

In 1914 these investors, worried about a possible German takeover, pressured Washington into sending the Marines to invade the island and protect their investments. The Marines stayed for twenty years, controlling Haiti until Franklin D. Roosevelt was elected and put an end to the occupation.

A Haitian strong man, Colonel Paul Magloire, seized power in 1950. His troops killed boys found with glue pots, on suspicion of putting up anti-Magloire posters. His genius consisted of talking Washington out of fifteen million dollars in foreign aid by convincing them of a Communist threat to Haiti. Later investigation revealed that this menace consisted exactly of one Communist chicken farmer who wrote novels. In December 1956, a general strike forced Magloire into exile.

One weak government succeeded another in the next nine months, each toppled by strikes and riots. Finally, François Duvalier, an obscure, American-educated former country doctor, engineered a fraudulent election and announced himself victorious. Taking over the National Palace, he declared martial law and began ruling as a dictator.

In January 1959, when revolution in Cuba brought Castro to power, a worried Washington decided to bolster Duvalier's shaky regime. A sixty-man Marine Corps unit was sent to Haiti to train and modernize the island's five-thousand-man army. Duvalier stood by while the Marines built this force for him. Then he turned it into a private army of hoodlum militia called by Haitians the Tonton Macoutes (Creole for "bogeymen").

To keep them personally loyal, Papa Doc let them shake down terrified businessmen for "taxes" and "donations." Instituting a reign of terror worse than any ever known in the Caribbean, the Macoutes crushed his enemies and silenced all critics. They halted busses, dragged off suspected peasants, and shot them on the spot. A night watchman who refused to let them pilfer supplies was found beaten to death, his body tied upright with barbed wire. Peasant women earning twenty cents a day selling vegetables at market were "taxed" half.

The American Embassy in Port-au-Prince, fed up with the grafting tactics of Duvalier's bogeymen, refused to let them control American gifts of food to hungry peasants. Papa Doc barred the food from leaving a port warehouse, where it rotted.

A rabid black nationalist, he used his gangsters to persecute Haiti's mulatto minority. One by one the island's doctors, lawyers, technicians, and businessmen were beaten and flung into prison or else they vanished mysteriously. About a hundred twenty-five thousand fled into exile. One of Papa Doc's ministers ventured to question the wisdom of losing all this precious talent for Haiti.

He suddenly found himself in prison, where he was tortured and half starved. Released six months later, he was embraced by a sobbing Duvalier. "Oh, my poor old friend!" wept Papa Doc. "They didn't tell me. It was all a mistake!" Poor Old Friend kept his mouth carefully shut from then on.

The dictator's reign of terror cost Haiti about eight million dollars spent annually by eighty thousand American tourists. The island's hotels soon grew empty when visitors arriving by air were searched by the Macoutes for concealed weapons, and those arriving by ship saw a fly-covered corpse tied to a chair on a pickup truck parked at the pier to remind Haitian dock workers in contact with Americans that silence was golden.

On May 7, 1961, Duvalier declared himself reelected to a new six-year term of office. One year later a new American President, John F. Kennedy, found it intolerable to continue United States support for a Caribbean ruler who had only a "Fascist answer" to the agonizing problems of his people. He stopped arms shipments to Duvalier, and in 1963 chopped off all aid except food relief and medical supplies. "We have stopped wasting our money," said a Kennedy official. Diplomatic relations with Haiti were also briefly suspended.

To prove that he was really the choice of his people, Papa Doc staged another phony election in April 1964. He was the only candidate. Eight hours before the polls closed, he appeared on a palace balcony to announce to the crowd collected by the Macoutes, "Citizen Dr. Francois Duvalier has won the battle. He has now been elected President-for-Life!"

His goal was to become a full emperor like Dessalines. On cue, mobs of Haitians were rounded up to cry out in front of the National Palace, "Long live the Emperor!" Once he persuaded Emperor Haile Selassie of Ethiopia to pay a state visit so that he could study how real emperors behaved.

Between 1964 and 1967 Duvalier survived two unsuccessful attempts by exiles to invade Haiti and overthrow him. His Macoutes tortured and beat to death all suspected sympathizers. One whole family of ten members, including an eighteen-month-old child, disappeared into Papa Doc's dungeons. He flooded the countryside with leaflets showing three severed heads and warning grimly, "Here is the fate awaiting all renegades!"

When two invaders were captured, he ordered all businesses and schools closed for a public holiday—an execution spectacle in the Port-au-Prince cemetery. After the execution, the Macoutes marched the crowd back to the National Palace to cheer for Papa Doc. He showed himself on the balcony, smiling and waving benignly.

While many regarded the satanic dictator as crazy, others regarded him as "crazy like a fox." Duvalier's people continued to be too crushed or terrified to rise up against him. Despite the death of nearly 30,000 people due to his repressive measures, Duvalier's reign lasted fourteen years, longer than any of his predecessors. Upon Duvalier's death in 1971, power transferred to his nineteen-year-old son, Jean-Claude, who was known as "Baby Doc" and who ruled until his overthrow in 1986.

8

Portugal

António de Oliveira Salazar (1889–1970)

The dictator of Portugal was as much a baffling paradox as the beautiful little country he ruled. Exploring Portugal in the 1960s, the author found hilltop castles and cathedrals, medieval walled cities, singing windmills, Roman ruins, pretty fishing villages with Phoenician half-moon boats, shepherds in sheepskin tunics, wine lodges, gorgeous red hills with cork trees blushing mauve like clipped poodles after a ninth-year shearing, white beaches, turquoise sea, lovely ancient cities dreaming beside lacy stone palaces.

Existence in this garden spot was sweet, tranquil, fragrant with flowers. Yet Portugal was tragically earth-poor. "We will be a rich country," Salazar once said ironically, "if the day comes when stones can be shipped abroad and sold by the pound." Portugal's people received less food, and had a higher tuberculosis death rate than any other Europeans. They had to work a day to earn what Scandinavians made in an hour.

In the north the farms were so tiny that families living on them could barely stay alive. In the south, four rich landowners possessed almost all the land and cork forests. Used to grinding poverty for centuries, most Portuguese were resigned to it and somehow managed to enjoy life despite it.

Startling contrasts were everywhere—luxury hotels and slum shacks; Cadillacs and donkeys; hydroelectric plants and fisherwomen in bare feet; a new Tagus bridge and fourteenth-century Moorish alleys; new schools and colleges and widespread illiteracy. This was Salazar's Portugal.

In the Constitution he gave the nation in 1933, he guaranteed freedom of speech, expression, worship, and association, and immunity from arbitrary arrest. But he also gave the government power to suspend these rights "in the cause of order." Many Portuguese freely criticized Salazar in private conversations, but seldom dared to in speeches.

Sometimes there were rumors of political murders, but Salazar denied them: "Some people think that from time to time we should have resorted to violence, which never does any good to any nation or any country. . . . Such revolutionary methods would be ill advised in our country. Violence does not suit the gentleness of our temperament and customs."

He brought stability and peace to a nation formerly torn by strife; but at a high price. "The people," he said, "have less need of being sovereign than of being governed." He saw his countrymen as charming but irresponsible children who needed his strong hand to control them. He forbade them to strike, considering this class warfare against private property. Management of the economy was put in the hands of Portugal's bankers, landowners, and industrialists, who controlled it through government corporations.

A true dictator, Salazar was nevertheless strikingly different from most. He came into office as Prime Minister by perfectly legal, honest means. A painfully shy and reserved man, he shrank from public ceremonies, acclaim, and publicity, preferring to live in lonely isolation. Authoritarian rather than totalitarian, he gave Portugal what has been described as Europe's only "police democracy."

Fifth child of a thrifty, hard-working peasant family, he was born in a small whitewashed cottage in the village of Vimieiro on April 28, 1889. Preferring books and long walks with his

António de Oliveira Salazar. (*Casa de Portugal*)

dog to playing games, he was a quiet, thoughtful "mama's boy." His mother's death left him inconsolable. "If she had not died," he once mused, "I wouldn't have become even a Minister. She couldn't have lived without me."

At eleven, he left the village school for his one chance at higher education—the seminary at Viseu. He proved so excellent a scholar that he won admission to the University of Coimbra in 1910, the year the army revolted against King Manuel and declared Portugal a republic. Coimbra students staged a wild celebration. As they smashed the furniture and fired shots into portraits of the King, Salazar quietly studied on.

For sixteen years, Portugal was torn by political chaos. In the name of democracy, there were twenty-four revolutions, 158 general strikes, forty-four changes of government. Salazar was sickened by the bomb-throwings, military revolts, naval mutinies, political arrests, assassinations, executions, strikes, and inflation. He joined a group of conservative students dedicated to restoring peace and order to the nation.

"A democracy cannot survive," he said in one speech, "when it grants privileges to one class of citizens at the expense of other classes. This is demagogy."

Winning a degree in political economy and finance, he joined the faculty at Coimbra in 1914. Four years later he was appointed a professor of economic sciences. His manner was so remote and chilly that he became known as "the man of ice." If a student attempted to shake hands after a lecture, he would step back and stare so severely that his admirer fled in panic. Living ascetically and frugally, he was a creature of habit who planned every hour of his day.

His writing and lectures on political economy began to attract national attention. In 1919, the government brought charges against him for teaching "monarchist propaganda," but they were dismissed upon his appeal to Portugal's High Court. Two years later he was persuaded to run for Parliament, and was one of three Catholic deputies elected.

Finding his opposition futile, however, he quit in disgust after only one day and returned to the university. It was more important, he felt, to teach Portugal's future leaders to exalt church and family, to practice self-discipline and financial frugality, both personal and national.

In 1926, the struggle for power in Portugal came to an end when General Manuel da Costa seized power and established a dictatorship. He asked the one Portuguese he knew to be honest, conservative, and a brilliant economist to become his Minister of Finance. The nation was bankrupt and needed a Salazar to put it on a sound financial basis.

Salazar demanded an austerity program that would impose heavy sacrifices upon the people. Fearful of revolution, da Costa refused. Salazar promptly quit and went back to Coimbra. Two years later, with the nation in utter financial chaos, he agreed to return to Lisbon on terms that gave him absolute control of the machinery of government.

He restored economic stability to Portugal, and on July 5, 1932, was rewarded with the post of Prime Minister. For his first cabinet he chose not politicians but professional experts—one engineer, one lawyer, one soldier. He had inherited the neglect of centuries. Industry was undeveloped; highways and railroads were dilapidated; civil service was an inefficient bureaucracy; the army was a rabble; there were few schools; Portugal's colonies were poorly governed.

Salazar sought to put a whole new foundation under Portugal by drafting a constitution called *Estado Novo* (New State), combining his ideas of social justice and authoritarian discipline. The economy was reorganized under a corporate system representing regions, industry, professions, and occupations. Salazar submitted the constitution to popular vote in 1933 by open ballot.

His balanced budget, forcing the nation to live within its meager means, caused increased hardship for most Portuguese.

But the people knew that at least Salazar practiced what he preached. He lived in three small rooms, eating frugally, buying his own coal, paying his servants out of his own $125-a-week salary. His stinginess became a national joke.

Restaurants offered "Codfish Salazar"—a wisp of fish with a few boiled potatoes. He was alleged to have his suits made without pockets so that he could not be begged for money. One story told of a minister seeking praise for economizing by running behind a streetcar instead of taking it. Salazar presumably snapped, "Run behind a taxi and save us *more!*"

"I am a prisoner," he once said mournfully. "With all my time and my thoughts devoted to the government, I have had to rule out any private life I might have." To ease his loneliness, he adopted two little girls. When one developed measles, he was at her side night and day. "It made me realize how wise I was in not caring for a family of my own," he said. "Otherwise I should have neglected Portugal."

He ran a quiet dictatorship behind the legal facade of a figurehead President. Absolute power was his, but it changed his way of life hardly at all. He preferred to spend time in seclusion, relaxing away from his desk in flower gardens or taking solitary walks through the countryside.

Hurt by a belief that his shy aloofness indicated a contempt for people, he once said defensively, "I'd rather be respected than loved." When grateful peasants showered him with gifts at the opening of a bridge he had built near their village, he told them coldly, "You don't have to thank me. I do everything to help you—nothing to please you!"

His sympathies were definitely Fascist. When the Spanish Civil War broke out in 1936, he sent a twenty-thousand-man Portuguese Legion to fight for Franco. He also purged Portugal's universities of "red intellectuals" who sympathized with the democratic government in Madrid. The following year he narrowly escaped being blown up in a chapel bombing.

A cautious man, he did not let his esteem for other dictators take him into World War II on the side of the Axis. In fact, when it became apparent, in October 1943, that Hitler was going to lose, Salazar shrewdly granted the Allies the use of the Azores as an air and naval base.

This gesture toward the democracies encouraged several thousand Portuguese to sign a petition urging free elections and a release of political prisoners. Salazar quietly turned the petition over to his secret police as a directory of "red intellectuals" to locate for "correction."

However, to win respectability among the democracies of the North Atlantic Treaty Organization (NATO), which Portugal had joined, he announced elections for 1949. When a political opponent took him seriously, Salazar denounced him as a public enemy, compelling him to withdraw his candidacy. This tactic was repeated in 1951. Each time Salazar's puppet President, Admiral Americo Thomaz, "won" easily at the polls.

Not until 1958 did an air force general, Humberto Delgado, dare defy Salazar by stumping the country to campaign against Thomaz. Rigging the election, the dictator declared Delgado the loser. The Bishop of Oporto angrily cried fraud. Salazar went on TV to announce he was abolishing popular elections and punishing all "agitators." Delgado prudently fled to Brazil. When he returned to Spain in 1965, to organize a coup, he was mysteriously murdered.

As Salzar fought to hold onto personal power, he also sought to hold onto Portugal's wide-flung colonial empire in a world where colonialism was rapidly breaking up. Without her colonies, symbols of her early greatness as a maritime power, Portugal would be reduced to a tiny country no more important than her meager home acreage. She would also lose raw cotton, sugar, vegetable oils, coffee, and sisal—an eighth of her imports, a quarter of her exports.

But the United Nations Trusteeship Council demanded that Salazar explain why Portuguese colonies used forced labor at twelve cents a day, denied political rights to natives, neglected to educate them for self-government, and flogged or tortured them for minor offenses. He angrily replied that it was none of the UN's business because the colonies were actually "overseas provinces" of Portugal. As for race relations, he pointed out, his government permitted no segregation or prejudice in the colonies, where it was said, "God created the white man and the black, but the Portuguese made the mulatto."

Late in 1960 over one hundred thousand Portuguese demonstrated in Lisbon in support of Salazar's position. A surprise opposition move came from overseas when Captain Henrique Galvão, a former official in Portuguese Angola who had escaped from imprisonment in Lisbon as a revolutionist, showed up in Brazil. To dramatize his opposition to Salazar, he turned pirate and captured the Portugese liner *Santa Maria*.

Meanwhile black nationalists in Angola led a fierce revolt. Burning Portuguese stores, they murdered and tortured colonists by blinding, flogging, and mutilation. Colonial police reacted with equal brutality, lynching natives and destroying villages with machine gun fire and napalm. Taking over the portfolio of Minister of Defense, Salazar rushed twenty-five thousand additional troops to Angola.

The Portuguese empire showed further signs of breaking up that year when India, tired of having a Portuguese colony on her soil, simply took over Goa. A few years later Red China, made it clear that Portuguese Macao would remain a colony only so long as it suited Peking.

To escape colonial service and domestic hard times, over a hundred fifty thousand Portuguese young men smuggled themselves illegally into France between 1959 and 1967. Salazar looked the other way because their remittances home from French paychecks brought Portugal an income of over forty million dollars a year.

In 1962 some dissatisfaction with the Salazar dictatorship finally erupted into the open. Antigovernment riots had to be dispersed by tear-gas bombs. Over a thousand students demonstrated against Salazar's ban on university free speech; most were arrested by police in a dawn raid.

But the vast majority of Portuguese continued to accept his rule philosophically. "What follows Salazar could be far worse," a Lisbon businessman told the author. "The country might fall back into chaos. That would give Franco the chance he has been waiting for—to swallow us up under the pretext of saving Portugal from Communism."

If Salazar's rule brought neither freedom nor democracy to Portugal, he did give his people a stable government and some improvement in their lives. They also respected him for living simply, refusing to take financial advantage of his position. "Before I leave my office," he said, "I shall turn my pockets inside out and shake them. I don't want to take anything with me, not even dust."

In 1968, Salazar suffered a stroke that incapacitated him and led to his removal from power. Although he survived for two years after the stroke, those close to him chose not to inform him of the change. Instead, they allowed him to "rule" in private until his death in July 1970.

9

Germany

Adolf Hitler (1889–1945)

At 12:38 P.M. on July 20, 1944, Colonel Claus von Stauffenberg carefully set down his briefcase under the conference table, five feet from Adolf Hitler in the dictator's field headquarters near Rastenberg. Ninety seconds later he excused himself to make a phone call. When a staff officer changed position at the table, his foot struck the briefcase. He moved it further from Hitler to get it out of the way.

Four seconds later the headquarters blew up.

Half the roof came down and the windows were blown out. Bodies flew into the air in an uprush of flames, black smoke billowing through the window frames and blown-out roof. SS men rushed into the ruins, carrying stretchers through the pall of smoke. One of those carried out was Adolf Hitler.

Word flashed to German generals involved in the conspiracy. Jubilant, they prepared to surrender Germany to the Allies and end the war Hitler had begun. But he was not dead. Hurled against the wall by the blast, he suffered only shock, face burns, and hearing injury. Foaming with rage, he shrieked orders to the Gestapo. Hundreds of army officers were seized, tortured, then hung by piano wire on meat hooks until they slowly strangled.

No, Adolf Hitler was far from dead. . . .

He was born on April 20, 1889, at Braunau in Upper Austria, third son of his father's third marriage. His father was a minor Austrian customs official whose name had originally been Schicklgruber. As a boy Hitler was pale, sickly, and shy, given to bursts of hysteria against anyone who disagreed with him. A poor scholar, he was a school dropout at sixteen.

Going to Vienna, he sought admission to the Academy of Fine Arts, but was rejected twice. For five years he drifted bitterly from one odd job to another. He copied and peddled picture postcards, shoveled snow, painted houses, beat carpets, worked as a railroad porter. Living in flophouses and eating in soup kitchens, he fumed at the "rich Jews" of Vienna as the cause of his failure and poverty.

"It was at this time that the greatest change took place in me that I was ever to experience," he wrote in his autobiography, *Mein Kampf (My Struggle)*. "From being a feeble world-citizen I became a fanatical anti-Semite. . . . Wherever I went I began to see Jews." In 1913 he left Vienna for Munich.

A failure here, too, he greeted the outbreak of World War I with relief. Eagerly joining the German infantry, he was delighted by the violence and excitement of war. His courage and enthusiasm as a message runner won him promotion to corporal and two awards of the Iron Cross. War's end found him hospitalized by a gas attack. He was stunned and dismayed by Germany's defeat.

A civilian-nobody once more, he prowled the streets of Munich in despair. His hatred for the new Weimar Republic knew no bounds. How *dare* those traitors admit German guilt for the war? How *dare* they sign the Versailles Treaty?

The German people were hungry. Allied troops roamed the streets of the Fatherland. Strikes had shut down factories everywhere. A brooding Hitler grew convinced that only a great German nationalist like himself could lead his "Aryan" nation out of postwar turmoil to its world destiny as "the master race." He turned to politics.

Adolf Hitler. (*National Archives*)

Joining the German Workers' Party, he quickly rose to a position of leadership. Under his influence it took on a paramilitary flavor, and was renamed the Nationalist Socialist German Workers' *(Nazi)* Party. Hitler used Mussolini's Blackshirts as a model for his party's uniformed strutting and street brawling. His early supporters included former fighter pilot Hermann Goering, political thug Ernst Roehm, student fanatic Rudolf Hess, and racist Alfred Rosenberg.

The Nazis made their move in 1923 when the German economy collapsed. Runaway inflation sent the price of a pound of meat from four marks to two billion. Capitalizing on nationwide panic, Hitler incited a crowd in a Munich beer hall and sought to lead them behind his Nazis in a *Putsch* against the government. The coup failed.

Tried for treason, he displayed open contempt for the court: "There is no such thing as high treason against the traitors of 1918!" His magnetic, forceful personality hypnotized crowds in the courtroom as he screamed imprecations at the "real enemies of Germany"—the French, the Jews, the pacifists, the Marxists, the German signers at Versailles.

As for his attempt to seize power: "The man who feels called upon to govern a people has no right to say, 'If you want me or summon me, I will cooperate.' No! It is his duty to step forward!" Sentenced to five years, he served only nine months. Influential supporters, furthermore, saw to it that he was jailed in great comfort with fine food and visitors.

It was here that he wrote his propaganda tract, *Mein Kampf,* the bible of Nazism. In it he frankly called for the extermination of Jewish and Slavic people; German expansion to the east through swallowing Russia; then world conquest to make Germany "lord of the earth." He praised Mussolini as one of the world's great men: "How dwarfish our sham statesmen in Germany appear in comparison with him!"

But when he wrote to Mussolini begging for a signed photo, the Italian dictator contemptuously replied through the Italian Embassy: "Il Duce does not think fit to accede to your request." Humiliated, Hitler never forgot the snub.

Released from prison, he held Nazi rallies to rant against his favorite targets until the irked Bavarian government forbade him to speak in public. "To this struggle of ours there are only two possible issues," he snarled. "Either the enemy passes over our bodies or we pass over theirs!" He began building the Nazi Party into a tightly disciplined private army. Many Germans laughed at the foolish Beer Hall Putsch gang and their ridiculous, mad leader.

World depression in the early thirties gave Hitler the chance he was waiting for. With German factories shut down and six million men jobless, Nazi ranks were swelled by the discontented. Through Josip Goebbels, a corrupt journalist, Hitler met steel tycoon Alfred Hugenberg and offered him a deal. If Hugenberg would get fellow industrialists to support the Nazis, Hitler would work to destroy the Weimar Republic and replace it with a strong anti-labor government dedicated to nationalism and militarism. Impressed with Hitler as an agitator and demagogue, Hugenberg agreed.

Now heavily financed, Hitler stepped up his propaganda, expanded his organization, and multiplied the squads of storm troopers who terrorized working-class districts by street warfare. His promises of a new, dynamic Germany won a large following among the lower-middle class. By 1932, he had captured more than a third of the popular vote.

When President Hindenburg invited him to become part of a coalition government, he refused coldly: "I must be chancellor—or nothing!" Pressure from Hugenberg and Franz von Papen, a powerful politician, finally compelled Hindenburg to name the former flophouse ne'er-do-well as chancellor of Germany. Hitler promptly began scheming to take power as absolute dictator.

On February 27, 1933, a demented Dutch youth set fire to the German *Reichstag* (Parliament). Hitler immediately denounced it as a Communist plot and declared martial law. He unleashed his Brownshirts, now a private army of two million, in a national wave of violence. They assaulted Jewish shopkeepers, crippled union leaders, broke into homes to hang anti-Nazis in their kitchens. Hitler held theatrical rallies in great public squares, making hysterical speeches to which huge crowds roared enthusiastically, "Sig *heil!*"

But his rise to total power was blocked by generals of the regular German Army. They suspected Hitler's Brownshirts of planning to usurp their military power. To ease their distrust and win their support, Hitler gave the signal for "the night of the long knives." On June 30, 1934, just after midnight, Brownshirt leader Ernst Roehm and all his aides were dragged from their beds and murdered in cold blood.

One month later President Hindenburg died. Satisfied they could trust Adolf Hitler, the German General Staff consented to his assuming the combined posts of Chancellor, President, and Army Commander-in-Chief. The German people were asked to vote approval of Adolf Hitler as their dictator. He won by an overwhelming vote of ninety per cent.

Some thirty-eight million Germans wanted Hitler to lead them.

He made sure they believed what he wanted them to believe, hated what he wanted them to hate. Josip Goebbels, his Propaganda Minister, followed Hitler's edict in *Mein Kampf:* "All propaganda should be popular and should adapt its intellectual level to the receptive ability of the *least* intellectual." The German people dutifully accepted his ban on all parties except the Nazis, and his censorship of press, radio, and schools. They attended his torchlight rallies, made bonfires of "dangerous books," roared their approval of the new Third Reich that "will last a thousand years."

We have no scruples!" he screamed proudly. "Yes, we are barbarians. We want to be barbarians. It is an honorable title!" He proceeded to prove the Nazi right to it.

In 1934, he ordered Austrian Nazis to murder their chancellor, Engelbert Dolfuss. The Nazi attempt to seize power was thwarted, however, when a worried Mussolini rushed troops to the Austrian border. Hitler sped to Venice to placate his former idol, but Mussolini snapped indignantly, "The trouble with Germans is they don't respect culture!"

"Culture!" snarled Hitler. "When I hear talk about culture, I have only one impulse—to draw my revolver!"

Mussolini told his wife, "The man's totally mad!"

In 1936 Hitler probed the determination of the League of Nations to stop aggression. He violated the Versailles Treaty by sending Nazi troops to seize and militarize the Rhineland. Allowed to get away with it, he began forging a world alliance of dictatorships, the Rome-Berlin-Tokyo Axis. The democracies watched uneasily as he and Mussolini sent tanks, planes, and troops to help Franco capture Spain.

In February 1938, Hitler suddenly annexed Austria and returned in triumph to Vienna, the city that had once ignored and humiliated him. A year later, despite British Prime Minister Chamberlain's feeble attempt to appease him at Munich, he seized Czechoslovakia. "It was our appendix" Goering explained cynically. "We had to cut it out."

Beside himself with joy, Hitler told his secretaries, "Children, kiss me! This is the greatest day of my life. I shall go down in history as the greatest of Germans!"

Next victim on his timetable was Poland. He disdained its alliance with England and France, convinced that the democracies would not go to war unless directly attacked. But what would Russia do if Nazi tanks swept up to its borders?

The world gasped when the fanatical anti-Communist urged Josip Stalin to sign a nonaggression pact. Stalin agreed, paving the way for a German declaration of war on Poland. Hitler's generals asked what pretext they should use.

"Any good propaganda reason will do," he said. "It doesn't have to be plausible. The victor will not be asked later on whether he told the truth or not." He had already justified the Nazi right to conquest in *Mein Kampf:* "Strength alone constitutes the right to possess."

When his attack on Poland finally provoked an Anglo-French declaration of war, Hitler's huge mechanized armies rolled through Denmark, Norway, Holland, Belgium, and then France, which fell in only a few weeks. He danced a gleeful little jig as he forced the French to surrender on the same spot as Germany had in 1918.

He began softening up Britain for invasion by saturation bombing. To his great rage, however, the English, their determination stiffened under the leadership of Winston Churchill, defied his "blitz" with great courage. Goering's air force failed to knock the RAF out of the skies over London, forcing Hitler to postpone invasion of England.

Frustrated, he unleashed his fury against the enemy he hated worst—Russia. Ignoring his pact with Stalin, he began "Operation Barbarossa" on June 22, 1941, so arrogantly sure of a quick victory that he sent his troops crashing into the Soviet Union without winter equipment or clothing.

In Hitler's new world order, there was no more room for Slavs than for Jews. He allowed no surrender of any besieged Soviet cities. "I want them wiped off the face of the earth!" he roared at his generals. As the Nazi war machine swept through Russia, some civilians were spared for slave labor or for use as guinea pigs in gruesome medical experiments. But millions of Soviet men, women, and children were murdered by firing squads, or exterminated in the gas chambers and ovens of Nazi death camps, along with millions of European Jews, intellectuals, and Marxists.

"Nature is cruel, therefore we too may be cruel," Hitler told Germans. "If I can send the flower of our nation into the hell of war, without the smallest pity for the spilling of precious German blood, then surely I have a right to remove millions of an inferior race that breeds like vermin!"

Convinced that he was a military genius, he refused to heed warnings by the German General Staff that the Nazi armies needed to retreat and regroup. "Never!" he screamed. "I will not yield one inch of ground! Attack, attack, always attack!" But all the great might of German armor failed to capture Stalingrad, Moscow, or Leningrad.

Then Stalin sprang his bear trap—a giant counteroffensive. One Nazi general whose division had been wiped out tried to hint to Hitler that his losses had been "unfortunately high." The Füehrer roared, "Losses can *never* be too high! They sow the seeds of future greatness!"

Disaster followed disaster. The English and Americans chased Rommel's forces out of North Africa, then knocked Italy out of the war. The Russians advanced on all fronts.

"My generals do not tell me the truth!" Hitler moaned to Goebbels. "They are all dishonest—all enemies of National Socialism! I get ill when I think of them!"

In 1944 when General Eisenhower opened the Second Front, liberating France, Hitler was stunned. The Third Reich that "will last a thousand years" was crumbling to pieces.

The attempt to assassinate him in July of 1944 embittered him against the whole German people. They had betrayed him, were unworthy of him! They deserved the nightly thunder of Allied bombs now dropping on their heads!

Like a deranged Nero, he seemed to have a pyromaniacal passion to see the whole world go up in flames along with his blasted hopes. As the Allies advanced on Paris, he ordered the city set afire; then he wired impatiently, "Is Paris burning?"

When the Russians began driving the Germans out of Poland, he screamed at General Franz Haider to raze Warsaw.

"His eyes popped out of his head," Haider recalled. "He was like a madman seized with a lust for blood."

As his nightmare world crashed down around his ears, Hitler retreated into a world of fantasy. He assured Mussolini that his "secret weapon"—the pilotless V-bombs he began hurling at London—would win the war for Germany. He ordered the Battle of the Bulge, telling Marshal von Rundstedt it would turn defeat into victory. He sent a special detachment of German commandoes, dressed in G.I. uniforms, to locate General Eisenhower in France and murder him.

His last desperate schemes failed. In 1945, as the Russians reached Berlin, he cowered gloomily in the underground bunker beneath his chancellery.

No longer the arrogant, self-appointed master of the world, he was now a complete psychopath, ulcerated, assailed by dizziness, racked by a convulsive twitch, addicted to drugs. He flew into hysterical fits of rage, screaming at any frustration from a lost battle to a pen that scratched.

He told his mistress, Eva Braun, who was in the bunker with him, that they must never be taken alive. As Russian troops burst into the outskirts of Berlin, he went through a wedding ceremony with her, than gave her poison and shot himself. Their bodies were burned, as he had demanded, on the chancellery grounds—the last blaze of the terrible Nazi holocaust he had unleashed upon the world.

The glum German people knew then what General Charles de Gaulle had meant when he had warned, "Dictatorship is a great adventure which crumbles in misery and blood."

10

Spain

Francisco Franco (1892–1975)

In 1949 Generalissimo Francisco Franco, dictator of Spain, fell into a choppy sea while fishing from his yacht *Azov*. A local Basque youth fishing from a nearby dory hastily dove to the rescue of the *Caudillo,* who couldn't swim. Rewarded with a medal and gift of money, he rushed home proudly to relate the story to his village.

"Jackass!" fumed his father. "Why didn't you let him drown? Heaven will never send us such a wonderful chance again!"

Son of a navy paymaster, Franco was born at El Ferrol, a naval base on the northwest tip of Spain, on December 4, 1892. He was given a military education, graduating at eighteen from the Toledo Academy as a second lieutenant. Promotions came swiftly while serving in Spanish Morocco. At twenty-three he was a major, at thirty-two a brigadier general, the youngest in Europe. The "baby general" compensated for his shrill voice, smallness, cherub face, and prissy manner by assuming a stiff-backed stance and a stony, ominous silence.

Once a burly Legionnaire, disgusted with the food served, threw a plate of it in Franco's face. The general calmly mopped his face and uniform with a handkerchief, then completed his inspection. Afterwards he issued three orders. The food was improved. The whole outfit was restricted to the garrison for three months. The soldier was shot.

Francisco Franco. (*Spanish National Tourist Office*)

Dull and unimaginative outside barracks, he was a shrewd and courageous tactician in battle. In 1920 he founded and commanded the first Spanish foreign legion, winning distinction by suppressing a Riff revolt. No carefree lover of wine and women like his men, he married the pious daughter of a wealthy Oviedo merchant. They had one child, a girl.

An archconservative, he supported King Alfonso his dictator, Primo de Rivera; and the Spanish Catholic Church, which had made blasphemy a criminal act and did not abolish the Inquisition formally until 1931. He was rewarded with command of the Saragossa Academy, where he told cadets, "The military life is not a road to pleasure and delight. It carries with it great sufferings, hardships, and sacrifices. Glory also, but like the rose it comes forth among thorns."

The world depression of 1931 swept away de Rivera's dictatorship, replacing it with an elected republic that began drawing up a constitution aimed at ending the Church's ancient privileges. The Cardinal-Primate of Spain called for full-scale opposition to the new government.

Riots swept the nation, with over a hundred churches set on fire. Franco's pro-Church academy was shut down, and he was transferred to an insignificant command in the Balearic Islands. His future looked bleak. But a struggle broke out for control of the Spanish Republic, with Left, Right and Center factions fighting each other for power. Spain slipped into revolutionary chaos. In 1934 the miners of Asturias began burning convents, shooting priests, and mistreating nuns.

The government sent for Franco. Leading Foreign Legionnaires against the miners, he killed five thousand and wounded thousands more. His massacre endeared him to conservative leaders, who made him chief of the army general staff.

However, early in 1936 the leftist Popular Front government of Manuel Azaña was elected. All army generals with monarchist or Church sympathies were transferred out of Spain. Exiled to the Canary Islands as a troop commander, Franco conspired with other exiled generals to overthrow the Republic.

Their rebellion began on July 17, 1936. A United States study of Fascism made for Congress by Representative Wright Patman of Texas revealed that their support came from monarchists, right-wing groups, the Church, big landowners, and bankers. Juan March, the richest man in Spain, exported Spanish ores to Hitler to secure tanks and arms for Franco.

Leading an army of Moorish troops and Spanish Legionnaires back to Spain, Franco proclaimed himself Chief of State. But the Spanish people, overwhelmingly behind the republic they had elected, formed a citizens' army to fight the generals. By July, Spain was divided in half. Franco's Nationalists controlled the north and west; Republican Loyalists held the south and east. Millions of Spaniards were weekend soldiers, working in fields and factories during the week, fighting in Loyalist lines on Saturday and Sunday.

A woman Communist known as La Pasionara pleaded with women to fight off the Fascists with knives and burning oil, crying, *"¡No pasarán!* They shall not pass! It is better to die on your feet than live on your knees!" Three thousand Madrid cab drivers volunteered a taxi brigade.

Franco had the help of fifty thousand Italian troops sent by Mussolini, and tanks and heavy artillery supplied by Hitler. The Axis powers also supplied bomber squadrons to test tactics for destroying cities and towns. "Everybody's with Franco," one correspondent reported wryly. "The Moors, the Germans, the Italians, everybody—except the Spanish people."

The Loyalists also had fighting with them an International Brigade composed of anti-Fascist volunteers from all over the world, later celebrated in novels by Ernest Hemingway and André Malraux. They understood the Spanish civil war to be a Fascist rehearsal for a world war to come. Franco's hatred for intellectual support of the Loyalists led him to raise the slogan: "Death to Intelligence!"

His naked brutality toward the Spanish people themselves so shocked priests in the Basque region that many helped the Loyalists, despite hierarchy support of Franco. Father Alberto de Onaindia was one stunned eyewitness to Franco's bombing of women and children in open cities.

On April 26, 1937, market day in Guernica, sacred town of the Basque region, Fascist bombers dropped explosives on the marketplace, machine-gunning peasants as they fled to the hills. Having taught the Basques a lesson for supporting the Loyalists, Franco then ordered fire bombs dropped on the martyred city, turning it into a blazing furnace.

"We were completely incapable of believing what we saw," said Father de Onaindia. "During the first hours of the night it was a most horrifying spectacle; men, women, and children were wandering through the woods in search of loved ones. In most cases they found only their bullet-riddled bodies."

The outrage shocked the world. Picasso, the famous artist, afterwards portrayed the scene in his masterpiece, the *Guernica*. Stung by world condemnation, Franco's propagandists charged that the Loyalists had committed their share of atrocities against captured Nationalists, and against priests and nuns supporting Franco.

It was a brutal war, with barbaric acts on both sides.

The Loyalist government received some help from the Soviet Union and Mexico, but the Western democracies refused to help, partly out of fear of challenging Hitler, partly out of reluctance to interfere in a civil war. Instead they "quarantined" the embattled nation, making it difficult to get supplies to the Loyalists while Franco continued to receive everything he needed from Germany and Italy.

The Spanish Government nevertheless fought stubbornly for three years, holding out longest in Madrid. It fell in March 1939, only after seven hundred thousand Spaniards had died in battle. Cities lay destroyed, industries were wrecked, agriculture was in ruins. But Franco's "New Order" had won the day.

He had himself proclaimed *Caudillo* (Chief of State for Life), Leader of the Empire, Commander in Chief of the Armed Forces, Prime Minister, Protector of the Church, head of the Falange, Spain's sole political party. The only title he did not claim was Dictator. He didn't have to.

"Spain," one Loyalist observed gloomily, "is now a country occupied by its own army." Franco converted convents, seminaries, bullrings, tobacco warehouses, and even universities into concentration camps and prisons for a half million Loyalist prisoners. His firing squads killed thirty thousand.

"I have never executed a man for fighting against me, nor for his political opinions" he assured British Field Marshal Sir Philip Chetwode in 1939. Disbelieved, he added lamely, "That is, not without giving him a trial first."

Regarding writers and intellectuals with sullen suspicion, he clamped total press censorship on Spain. Literacy was discouraged by reducing teachers to starvation wages; college professors were slashed to twenty-five dollars a week. Forbidding strikes, he collected twenty-five million dollars in taxes on workers' wages, but only two million dollars in taxes from Spain's wealthy classes.

When World War II broke out, he repaid Axis help by sending the Spanish "Blue Division"—forty-seven thousand "volunteers"—to fight beside the Nazis in Russia. "Spanish blood is flowing in this noble enterprise," he declared proudly. Upon the fall of France, he met Hitler on the French-Spanish border to congratulate him. Later he wrote, "Dear Füehrer: I stand ready at your side . . . decidedly at your disposal, united in common historical destiny." His enthusiasm cooled, however, as it became apparent that Hitler faced disaster.

Franco craftily resisted German pressure to enter the war officially, even after Hitler spent nine hours trying to persuade him. "Rather than go through that again," Hitler groaned to Mussolini, "I'd prefer to have three or four teeth yanked out." He cursed Franco as a jackal.

The Spanish dictator's obvious Axis sympathies hardly endeared him to the Allies. At Potsdam, Churchill revealed that Franco had tried to get him to switch the war against "that terrible country Russia." President Truman related, "I made it clear that I had no love for Franco." The first United Nations General Assembly recommended to all nations that they withdraw their ambassadors from Spain.

Franco sat tight, aware that the Spanish people—however much they might despise him—would proudly resent outside pressure on Spain. His dictatorship remained isolated until 1953, when President Eisenhower decided that United States security required air bases in Spain, and paid Franco a personal visit. Suddenly "respectable," the dictator quickly agreed to a deal that pumped billions of American dollars into the Spanish economy and won him admission into the United Nations.

That same year he re-established the Church as the dominant factor in Spanish life with an annual subsidy of over five million dollars and far more power than it had ever had even under the Catholic kings. But some Church leaders were not too happy with a concordat that obliged them to support a police state. They deplored the government syndicates that pretended to speak for workers and students, but whose real function was to stifle protest and prevent opposition.

In 1956, students at Madrid University held a demonstration to demand an end to the syndicates. Police and Falangist thugs beat the marchers senseless. One student was shot, hundreds arrested. Franco fired his Education Minister for not having headed off the demonstration.

He ordered Madrid cafes to stop serving food after midnight, to drive students to bed early, thus emulating Franco himself. He set them an example by sometimes praying in his chapel for hours. They remained singularly unimpressed with the piety of the dictator whose face was engraved on every Spanish coin with the description: "Chief of State by the Grace of God."

On the twenty-fifth anniversary of his rise to power, Franco ordered a huge celebration. To show his magnanimity, he invited political refugees to return to Spain, and pardoned all political prisoners who had served twenty years.

Increasing tourism, foreign investments, and United States aid brought prosperity to Spain's middle class. Franco's wealthy colonels and generals sat on all the boards of directors of the banks and corporations. Five million peasants still harvested crops with only hand tools on land owned by absentee land-lords, and coal miners made nine dollars a week.

"Something between eighty and ninety per cent of the people as a whole oppose Franco," famous author John Gunther reported in 1961, "but they have no means of displacing him."

A year later the coal miners of Asturias, whom Franco had once massacred by the thousands, struck illegally. The walkout spread to mines, factories, and shipyards all over Spain until one hundred thousand workers had put down their tools. Franco rushed armed police to three northern provinces, proclaiming a state of emergency and suspending civil rights.

"The only time we hear about civil rights," one miner said, "is when they're suspended." A student explained to London correspondent Alexander Werth how Franco's regime of "Freedom and Order" operated: "Freedom says something it shouldn't say—and Order socks it between the eyes!"

The dictator was shaken when Spain's leading Roman Catholic magazine came out in favor of the strikers. The Church was becoming increasingly disenchanted with Francoism. A petition by 352 Basque priests condemned his suppression of freedom. Some Catholic archbishops insisted that he end press censorship. One priest explained, "We are concerned that the Church may be nailed into Franco's coffin."

Furious, Franco ordered rough treatment for priests supporting the strikers; three were even arrested. He was reproved by powerful Cardinal Pla y Deniel, who pointed out that social justice was in accord with Catholic teaching, but that idolatry of the state was *not*. To settle the strike, Franco was finally forced to accept the workers' demands. In a black mood he fired his Minister of Labor.

That summer bombs blew up a bank and newspaper offices in Madrid and Barcelona. One explosion outside Franco's summer palace near San Sebastian shattered windows. His press ran furious headlines: TREASON AND STUPIDITY ARE ALLIED IN A DIRTY UNION AGAINST SPAIN. Police arrested dozens of political suspects, executing one and exiling others.

Foreign correspondents speculated about a revolution. One former Loyalist said sadly, "We can't start another civil war. People of my generation are too scared of war."

The success of the miners encouraged university students to hold protest demonstrations against Franco's education policies. Over nine thousand Spanish municipalities had no public libraries. School budgets were so miserly that science students were allowed only one experiment each semester. Government syndicates still held students captive. Whenever they dared protest, security police brutally smashed the demonstrations.

Forced to flee in Barcelona, the students were sheltered in a Capuchin monastery. Franco angrily cut off the monastery's essential services. For two days monks and students held out on a diet of thin asparagus soup. On the third day police stormed the monastery and made arrests. By 1967 furious students were raising a new battle cry: "Dictatorship, No! Democracy, Yes!" Franco shut down Barcelona and Madrid universities.

Growing uneasy at rising unrest over his tyranny, Franco sought to placate his opposition with a token concession. He offered to let twenty percent of Spain's governing body be elected by popular vote. Submitting this "plebiscite" to the Spanish people in a controlled election, he claimed his "victory" as a vote of public confidence.

But he was no longer so sure of his old power to rule by inspiring terror. In 1967 police arrested six electrical workers in

Madrid for taking part in a protest march. The plant's thirteen thousand workers simply folded their arms at their benches. Franco quickly got the message. As soon as the six workers were released, work began.

"Yes, we were frightened," one leader of the sitdown admitted to an American reporter. "But frightened or not, the only way is forward. There is no turning back now!"

In 1969, already in his late seventies, Franco designated Prince Juan Carlos, the grandson of King Alfonso XIII, as his official successor upon his death. Despite his plan to reinstitute rule by monarchy, Franco believed that much of the authoritarian regime he had built would last. Yet after Franco's death in 1975, Juan Carlos moved to dismantle the authoritarian institutions of Franco's system. He encouraged the return of political parties and ratified a new constitution that made Spain a democratic constitutional monarchy, which it remains today.

II

Indonesia

Achmed Sukarno (1901–1970)

Young Achmed Sukarno saw nothing wrong in cheating on school exams. "It falls under the heading of what we call cooperation," he explained. Fiercely competitive, he never allowed himself to be eclipsed. "In the game of spinning tops, a friend's top once spun faster than mine," he recalled. "I solved the situation with typical Sukarno quick thinking—I threw his top in the river!" His logic did not change much as ruler of a million Indonesians.

He was born June 6, 1901, in Surabaya, eastern Java. His father was a schoolteacher, his mother a proud Balinese convinced that her son had the mark of destiny upon him.

"You are a child of the dawn," she told him. "You will be a man of glory, a great leader of your people." He believed it, but was troubled by the scorn of Dutch children who snubbed him as a dark-skinned native. As a teenager he wooed and won Dutch girls by his good looks and eloquence: "It was the only way I knew to exert some form of superiority over the white race, and make them bend to my will!" He grew into an incorrigible ladies' man, marrying four times without the bother of any divorces in between.

At fifteen he joined a secret nationalist party sworn to throw the Dutch out of Indonesia. In three centuries of colonial rule, the Netherlands had derived great riches from the three thousand islands spanning an area as wide as the United States. Enrolling as an engineering student in the Bandung Institute of Technology, Sukarno studied revolution through the eyes of Garibaldi, Danton, Marx, and Lenin. His idols, however, represented an odd assortment of influences—Hitler, Mussolini, Roosevelt, George Washington, and Mohammed.

Graduating in 1926, he shelved his degree in civil engineering to make inflammatory political speeches. Only five feet four, he was an eloquent giant on a speaker's platform, fluent in English, German, French, and Dutch. Crowds were inspired by his call for "democratic socialism"—a Sukarno political cocktail with equal parts of the Spirit of 1776, Islam, Christianity, and Karl Marx.

In July 1927, he organized the Indonesian Nationalist Party (PNI). Its motto, "Complete Independence—Now!", was not appreciated by the Dutch, who ordered it disbanded. Sukarno refused and spent most of the next thirteen years in prison. As a martyred leader of the freedom movement, he inspired the same kind of love and reverence among his people that Indians had felt for an imprisoned Gandhi.

They called him Bung (Brother) Karno. It was not he, however, but the Japanese who threw the Dutch out of Indonesia. When they swept through the Pacific in 1942, he was found exiled on Sumatra. He welcomed the Japanese as deliverers and was allowed to act as a puppet President to pacify Indonesia for them. He hinted to his people that he was cooperating with the Japanese only until he could get rid of them.

When it became clear that they were about to go down in defeat, Sukarno made his move. Just before August 1945, he seized stores of Japanese arms and ammunition, proclaiming a "Republic of Indonesia" with he himself as President. But when the war ended, Allied forces returned Indonesia to the Dutch, who refused to deal with Sukarno. Four years of guerrilla warfare ended in his capture and internment.

Achmed Sukarno. (*United Nations*)

In 1949, however, United Nations pressure forced the Dutch to end their colonial rule. Sukarno popped to the surface once again like an irrepressible cork as President and Premier of the new Republic. For eight years he led a parliamentary democracy, his executive powers held in check by representatives of the nation's three thousand islands. One of his accomplishments was a crash program of popular education, reducing Indonesian illiteracy from ninety-three to forty-five per cent.

Little by little he moved the Republic toward the Left, under the influence of the PKI, a Marxist organization with close ties to Red China. Its leader was a revolutionary named Aidit, who shrewdly played on Sukarno's vanity by calling upon Indonesians to revere him as "Great Leader of the Revolution," "Savior of Indonesia," and "Supreme Peasant." Aidit always turned the PKI out in force to cheer Sukarno's speeches. "The PKI gets things done," Sukarno reproached other political leaders. "All of you should be more like them!"

His self-esteem knew no limits. "I love my country and I love women," he declared, "but most of all I love myself!" Once he showed up for a palace press conference in a brilliant sky-blue marshal's uniform—and bare feet. A correspondent asked why. "An electric storm is brewing," he replied seriously. "I want to build up my energy. I absorb electric impulses from the ground."

In 1956 he paid a state visit to Washington, where President Eisenhower received him formally but unenthusiastically. Ever suspicious of the white West, Sukarno felt snubbed. He was given a cordial welcome in Moscow, however, where the Russians deepened his conviction that only Marxism had the answer for a colored race with vast wealth in rubber, oil, and tin, but a per capita income of only sixty dollars a year.

Returning home, he branded the parliamentary democracy of Indonesia a failure. "I can't and won't ride a three-legged horse!" he vowed. He announced a new "guided democracy," which turned out to mean suspending the elected Parliament and setting up a personal dictatorship.

The two most powerful forces in Indonesia were the army and the Communist Party. Playing off one against the other so that he could pose as savior-above-the-battle, he cleverly united them behind him in common hatred of the Dutch. Confiscating Dutch investments, he demanded that the Netherlands government turn over neighboring West Irian (Dutch New Guinea). To emphasize the threat, he ordered a hundred twenty million dollars' worth of United States arms, but Washington prevented the sale.

Secretary of State John Foster Dulles was nervous about Sukarno's move to the Left. Would America's half-billion dollar investments in Indonesian oil, rubber, and tin be confiscated next? Would a Red Indonesia lead to the spread of Communism throughout Southeast Asia? Dulles decided to go along with a secret CIA plot to get rid of Sukarno,

In December 1957, soldier of fortune Allen Pope was hired to fly U.S.-armed Indonesian exiles from Manila to the North Celebes, where they set up a rival Indonesian government on Sumatra and called upon the army to revolt.

"There is no cause for alarm or anxiety," Sukarno soothed his followers. But he rushed reliable army forces to Sumatra to crush the rebels, who made the mistake of appealing publicly for United States recognition and more arms. An embarrassed Dulles replied with a public protest of neutrality.

Buying a hundred planes and other arms from Communist East Europe, Sukarno bitterly accused Washington of having supplied the rebels with planes, automatic weapons, and ammunition. When his accusation was denied, a trump card fell into his hands. Allen Pope was shot down as he flew a bombing mission for the rebels. Red-faced Washington officials moved swiftly to "improve relations" with Sukarno by suddenly offering to sell him rice, small arms, and plane parts.

However, outraged Indonesian generals insisted that Pope be tried before a military court, where he was found guilty and sentenced to death. A new United States President, however, invited Sukarno to Washington. He warmed up to John F. Kennedy when the President told a White House aide, "No wonder Sukarno doesn't like us very much. He has to sit down with people who tried to overthrow him!"

Six months later, with the rebellion in Sumatra crushed, Sukarno quietly released Pope from prison and allowed him to fly back to the United States. He was rewarded with millions of dollars' worth of aid and loans for his sagging economy from a United States hopeful of wooing him from Communism.

But Sukarno was bored and restless unless he was in the spotlight. "Continuing revolution" appealed to him as an exciting pastime. "We have made a complete break with Western democracy," he shouted to crowds. "Let Nekolim abroad be in an uproar!" For easier sloganeering, he coined words like "Nekolim"—"neocolonialism and imperialism."

His flamboyant grandstanding in a snow-white uniform, wearing dark sunglasses and carrying a swagger stick, provoked scorn in political opponents. Privately, they sneered at the *Bapak* (father) of Indonesian freedom as a demagogue. Stung, he snapped, "If I were indeed just a demagogue, why would they be afraid of my demagoguery?" He felt secure as long as he controlled the three-hundred-fifty-thousand-man army with its Russian equipment, and had the support of Indonesia's three million Communists. As relations began warming up between Moscow and Washington, Sukarno retrimmed Indonesian sails to Red Chinese weather. His Leftist foreign minister, Subandrio, negotiated with Premier Chou En-lai to substitute Chinese influence for Russian. But the nation's Muslims grew increasingly unhappy with Sukarno's move to the extreme Left. Between 1957 and 1962, a fanatical Islam sect made five attempts to kill him. Sukarno tried to blame the Dutch.

He had sent a small paratroop force into West Irian to seize it from the Netherlands. It was of little value to anyone, but Sukarno needed it to bolster his prestige. Like most dictators who don't know what to do about economic troubles, he turned to foreign conquest to drown out criticism under an aroused patriotic fervor. As Plato observed about the dictator, "He is always stirring up some war or other, in order that the people may require a leader."

He was delighted when the United Nations hesitantly agreed to transfer the mandate of West Irian to Indonesia. Next on his timetable was the "liberation" of Malaya, Singapore, and Borneo from British colonialism. He was dismayed when London gave these possessions their independence, uniting them first in the new nation of Malaysia. Denouncing it as a British puppet, Sukarno shouted to his people: "Crush Malaysia!"

In January 1964, even as his troops attacked, Malaysia was elected to a seat on the United Nations Security Council—a diplomatic slap in the face for Sukarno. Playing on his wounded vanity, Aidit and Subandrio worked him up to a fit of rage until he made the grand gesture of taking Indonesia out of the United Nations. He called upon other anticolonial nations to follow his exit. To his chagrin, not one did.

He made wild speeches attacking UN aid programs: "What is UNICEF? It is powdered milk. I prefer to eat cassava [a flour-yielding root]. FAO [the Food and Agriculture Organization] sends experts who know nothing about Indonesia's agriculture. I say to them, 'To hell with your aid!'" His substitution of personal temper tantrums for international diplomacy worsened the economic plight of Indonesia by cutting it off from the rest of the world.

Tin and rubber production fell off sharply. Roads and railroads built by the Dutch fell into disrepair. Inflation doubled prices in six months, adding half-naked children to thousands of starving Indonesians begging in the streets. Sukarno insisted upon spending two-thirds of the national budget on the army's operations against Malaysia. When his ministers gingerly tried to discuss the country's financial plight, he groaned, "Economics makes my head ache!"

United States support of Malaysia gave him a chance to use Washington as a scapegoat for his failures. He threatened seizure of U.S. oil and rubber investments; he boycotted American films and kicked out the popular Peace Corps. PKI goon squads attacked the U.S. Embassy and island consulates, and forced American libraries to shut down. Warned of a cutoff of United States aid funds, Sukarno screamed, "To hell with your aid!"

With rice scarce, he ordered Indonesians to cultivate a taste for corn and sweet potatoes. Aidit offered him a suggestion for a better protein diet combined with pest control: "If the peasants start eating rats eagerly, the rats will be wiped out, and there will even be a rat shortage."

In February 1965, Sukarno confiscated U.S. rubber plantations worth eighty million dollars in Sumatra "to protect them from angry workers." He stopped the mail of Americans living in Djakarta and advised their servants to quit. The PKI staged riotous anti-United States, pro-Peking demonstrations.

Anti-Communist army leaders, led by Moslem Defense Minister Nasution, met secretly and decided that the time had come to stop Sukarno's moves to make Indonesia a Red Chinese satellite. Posters began appearing all over Djakarta: "Hang Foreign Minister Subandrio!" Nasution threw Communist officials out of his ministry, and forced the suspension of fifty-seven Communist members of Parliament. Then he charged Subandrio with plotting a Communist coup in Indonesia.

Army commanders loyal to Subandrio and Aidit suddenly kidnaped Nasution and his top generals, six of whom were murdered.

They missed General Suharto, who surrounded the palace with paratroop battalions. Sukarno left hastily to join Aidit at Halim Air Force Base. "The best place for me," he admitted later, "was near an airplane." Aidit urged him to set up a "Revolutionary Council," but he hesitated.

Suharto took command of the government and ordered a ruthless anti-Communist purge all over Indonesia. Confused and desperate, Sukarno shouted to all factions, "Leave it to me! Leave it to Bapak!" But it was too late. Aidit was seized and shot. In Central and East Java thousands of Communists and their families were massacred. Army and Muslim groups slaughtered an estimated one hundred thousand Indonesians.

Sukarno pleaded with his people to stop fighting among themselves and unite against "our real enemy—the Nekolim!" They were still personally fond of him, but felt he had been a dupe of the Reds and needed "correction" by the army.

"How can I solve the September 30 incident," he whined, referring to the date of the attempted Communist coup when Nasution and his generals were kidnapped, "if my people pay me no heed?" He bristled at Nasution's demand that he reverse Indonesia's foreign policy, shouting, "I am *still* President, *still* Great Leader of the Revolution, and will not retreat from my policies by one inch!"

Huge student demonstrations demanded an end to the dictator's rule of chaos, mismanagement, and corruption. On March 11, 1966, Suharto's troops seized the palace, arresting Sukarno and Subandrio. Sukarno was forced to sign a decree giving full powers to Suharto. Subandrio was tried for treason and sentenced to a firing squad "for having brought tragedy to Indonesia and misery to all layers of the community." Everyone knew he was being made the goat for Sukarno.

Sukarno was safe for the moment because, as one local commander explained, "The people still feel that he is their father, and a child feels that he must defend his father even if he has done something terribly wrong." He was stripped of all titles except that of Bapak, and permitted to remain in the palace as a figurehead.

The blow to the vanity of "the George Washington of Indonesia" was shattering. He kept denying that he had lost power, putting up a cocky front in public: "Here I am, always smiling . . . still the leader of the revolution!" When reporters pressed him for clarification, he snapped, "I'm shutting my mouth in a thousand languages!" Issuing orders no one obeyed, making pronouncements nobody heeded, he grew moody and depressed. He began to plead for understanding.

"People sometimes make mistakes," he whined, "and if you show what my mistakes are, I shall correct myself."

In early 1967, Indonesia's new strong man, Suharto, gave the fallen dictator an ultimatum—exile or trial for treason. And so Sukarno faded from public view—not with a bang but a whimper.

"He is both loved and despised—a tragic figure," observed a European businessman in Djakarta. "But for all his faults there never was anyone like Sukarno in Asia, nor is there likely ever to be anyone like him again."

Yugoslavia

Josip Broz Tito (1892–1980)

Whoomp. The four guerrilla leaders of the Partisan General Staff flung themselves to earth. *Whoomp-whoomp-whoomp.* A smoky blast of dirt, steel, and stones cascaded over them as a second German bomber screamed low overhead.

Tito looked up. "They've spotted us, all right. We've got to get out of the mountains. Quickly."

"We have three thousand wounded and sick, Comrade," protested his lieutenant, Milovan Djilas. "How can we carry them out?"

"Arm them. Let them fight their way out with us. It's better than risking capture and torture by the Nazis!"

The Germans launched their all-out offensive to clear the Yugoslav Partisans out of the Grmeč Mountains on January 15, 1943. Tito moved his columns south, single file. Strafed constantly, pitifully short of food and medical supplies, freezing in bitter winter winds, they fought through heavy snowdrifts and river torrents to escape Nazi encirclement. Tito shared their suffering, eating the same horse meat, going hungry when they did. He radioed constant pleas to Moscow for airdrops of food, medicine, and ammunition.

Stalin always replied with eloquent praise for their heroic fight—and regrets. Tito was left to stand off the powerful

Josip Broz Tito. (*United Nations*)

German Army with only three bullets per Partisan. The Nazis laughed at Tito's forces as "three-bullet men."

He wondered grimly whether Stalin was sacrificing the Partisans to prove to Churchill and Roosevelt that he had no interest in supporting any Communist Party outside Soviet borders. Stalin had even told Tito to take red stars off his guerrilla's caps, asking, "Why frighten the British?" Significantly, Moscow had also failed to denounce the Yugoslav Chetniks, royalist troops led by Mihailovich who were fighting the Partisans instead of the German invaders.

Was it possible, Tito brooded, that the cause to which he had devoted his whole life—international Communism—was betraying him? His growing disillusionment with Moscow was to have world-shaking consequences at war's end.

He was unswerving in his own fidelity to Socialist principles. One day a sick Partisan was brought before him for an "act of sabotage"—scratching oats out of a peasant's field. "You know we depend upon peasant support," Tito said harshly. "How can you possibly excuse such theft?"

"I was starving," the Partisan whispered.

Tito's eyes blurred. But he clenched his jaw and ordered the man shot. Bandaging the doomed man's eyes himself, he muttered, "You must forgive me, Comrade. If we permit crimes against our own people, they will soon find us no better than the Germans or the Chetniks."

Thin, pale, exhausted, he strove to keep himself looking presentable. "It reassures the soldiers," he told his Partisan wife, "to see their commander shaved and groomed."

He astonished the pursuing Germans by suddenly turning on their flanks with fierce hit-and-run attacks. Capturing fifteen tanks, heavy artillery, and many prisoners, he escaped through German lines in a fierce battle that cost many Partisan lives. An enraged Hitler sent seven fresh German divisions, trained in mountain warfare, to finish him off.

Outnumbered six to one, his seventy-third radio appeal for aid to Moscow ignored, Tito sent an S.O.S. to the Allied Command in the West. General Dwight Eisenhower, who admired his gallant struggle against the Nazis, airdropped supplies to the Partisans. Tito never forgot who had helped him.

On June 9, 1943, Stukas located his mountain headquarters and dropped fragmentation bombs. Many around Tito were killed; he was blown into the air by concussion and wounded in the left arm. Putting it in a sling, he escaped Nazi divisions closing in by leading his guerrillas up almost perpendicular limestone cliffs, a four-thousand-foot climb.

Retreating through the craggy Maglich, their ranks were clogged by one hundred thousand refugees, many of whom starved or froze to death in the bitter mountain nights. Tito's aides urged him to leave the civilians behind: speed was imperative.

"Never!" he snapped. "If we abandon our people to be massacred by the Germans, what are we fighting for?"

Pursued by mortar blasts and the crash of howitzer shells, they survived by eating their pack ponies, then beech tree leaves. Hitler's forces encircled them. Tito decided that their one chance to break out was to attack the most lightly held position on the perimeter, even though it meant charging across an open valley. His aides protested that German fire would rip them to pieces.

"Not if we run fast enough," he replied grimly. Hundreds of Partisans fell before a storm of shellfire, mortars, and machine-gun crossfire. Their comrades raced over their bodies, overrunning Nazi gun emplacements and fighting fierce hand-to-hand battles. Then the surviving Partisans escaped through the hole punched in the ring of steel.

The Germans were never able to crush Tito and his Partisans. He came out of the war a great national hero and a Communist leader who owed nothing to Josip Stalin.

Josip Broz Tito was perhaps the most unusual Red dictator in the world—tough, independent, cool in danger, audaciously brave, flexible in tactics but unswerving in principle, sincerely devoted to his people, friendly to the West.

His birth at Kumrovec, Croatia, part of the Austro-Hungarian empire, took place on May 25, 1892. He was one of fifteen brothers and sisters, eight of whom died in childhood for lack of proper food and medical care. The older children shared an upstairs garret, the smaller ones slept on rags on the floor. His father farmed, did blacksmith work, and hauled wood up the mountains. Tito was apprenticed to a locksmith, and afterwards became a metal worker.

When World War I broke out he was forced to fight in the Austrian Army, although at twenty-two he already belonged to a secret antiroyalist workers' movement. Wounded on the Carpathian front, he was taken prisoner of war by the Tsar's army in March 1915. He taught himself Russian and read Tolstoy, Dostoevsky, and Gorky while he waited for the war to end.

When he gained his freedom, he joined the Red Army and fought in the civil war against White Russians. A rout in enemy territory sent him into hiding. Sheltered by a Russian girl, whom he later married, he escaped to the steppes and joined a nomadic tribe of fierce Kirghiz horsemen. He broke horses and hunted wolves with them until it was safe to return to his wife and take her back to Yugoslavia.

In 1920 he found his country an independent nation set up by the Versailles Treaty. As a Croat he resented the Serb government, which oppressed the Croat minority. Joining the Yugoslav Communist Party, he was frequently jailed for agitating among shipyard and railway workers.

The nation fell into an uproar over the political murder of Croat leaders in 1929. Tito distributed arms to Croat nationalists, and once escaped Serb police by jumping out of a first-floor window onto a table loaded with pork. When the police finally cornered him and found bombs in his flat, they kept him awake for eight days and nights of violent interrogation. He refused to talk and defied the judge at his trial: "I recognize no authority but that of the Communist Party!"

During his five-year sentence, an army revolt overturned the Serb government and put King Alexander on the throne. When he was freed, Royalist police banned him from all towns as a dangerous radical. This was the last straw for his wife, who went back to Russia. Tito took to the woods and mountains, where he built so strong a Communist movement that Moscow made him Party chief in Yugoslavia.

In 1941, Hitler invaded the Balkans to "mop up" his rear before attacking Russia. Tito organized his followers into a Yugoslav National Liberation Army. However, the British recognized only the royalist Mihailovich, until Winston Churchill's son Randolph parachuted into Tito's mountain headquarters. He found the Partisans superbly disciplined. Tito permitted no looting, drinking, or romantic entanglements with women Partisans. The nation's diverse racial and religious groups, once in conflict, were united behind the Partisans.

Young Churchill's glowing report persuaded his father to switch England's support to Tito. The Prime Minister asked a "small favor" in return when he met Tito in Italy in August 1944—to let Peter, son of the murdered King Alexander, come to the throne after the Nazis were driven out. Stalin told Tito privately, "You don't have to restore the King forever, you know. Just take him back temporarily, then slip a knife into his back at a suitable moment."

"No," Tito replied. "The Kerensky regime made a mistake in 1917 by aiming at democracy first, socialism afterwards. My policy is socialism first, democracy afterwards. And *my* democracy won't be Western style—with only two parties, both alike and both run by and for big business!"

On March 7, 1945, Tito, by now a self-appointed marshal, became Prime Minister of Yugoslavia. To help him rebuild his war-shattered country, the United Nations sent him a half billion dollars in aid, seventy percent of it American funds. Tito was indignant when Washington hinted this aid might be cut off if he failed to align Yugoslavia with the Western powers.

"No one is going to buy me or my country!" he snapped. "It is ironic that more aid is now going to defeated Germany—the enemy who invaded Yugoslavia—than to us, the victims of the Nazis. If U.S. dollars come only with political strings attached to them, the United States can keep them!"

He took an equally independent attitude toward Moscow, which he had never forgiven for its failure to help the Partisans in their hour of need. When he coolly rejected a Kremlin plan for tailoring Yugoslavia's economy to meet Soviet needs, Stalin summoned him to Moscow to lay down the law.

At a Kremlin party Stalin boasted, "Careful, there's still strength in me!" He lifted the tough Yugoslav leader off the floor three times, to the beat of a Russian folk tune. Toasting Tito, he added ominously, "Notice I call you Comrade, not Mister . . . *yet*" It was a thinly veiled threat to read Tito out of the world Communist movement.

"In the teachings of Marx, Engels, Lenin, *and* Stalin," Tito replied defiantly, "we are the equals of the Russians."

He made clear his intention to build an independent brand of socialism in Yugoslavia. His courageous conviction that all Communist countries had the right to plan their own destinies, and his successful example, was not lost on other dissatisfied Red regimes behind the Iron Curtain.

Hungary went into open revolt and had to be crushed by Soviet tanks, a severe blow to Russian prestige. Other East Europe leaders began demanding increased freedom from Moscow control. Khrushchev and the present Soviet leaders had to develop a new relaxed foreign policy to placate them. It was Tito more than anyone else who had forced an end to Stalin's Cold War, and rolled back the Iron Curtain.

Washington had second thoughts about the plucky Yugoslav who had made it clear that, Communist or not, he was nobody's pawn. Eisenhower offered Tito aid on his own terms—no strings—in the form of a billion dollars' worth of food and machinery. Tito began rebuilding his nation's economy into what Yugoslav wits called "capitalism without capitalists." The two leaders met at the United Nations in September 1960.

"He was shorter than I had expected, and reserved," the President related. "In contrast to Khrushchev, he was a good listener. . . . He made quite a point of the affection that the Yugoslavs feel for the United States because of our help to them during World War II."

Khrushchev tried to woo Tito back into the Kremlin camp by admitting that Stalin's expulsion of Tito from the Cominform in 1948 had been a blunder. But the Yugoslav dictator was now firmly committed to a new policy—neutralism. He called a meeting of other neutral nations at Belgrade in September 1961 to develop a third force to stand between the two Goliaths, the U.S. and USSR, and keep world peace.

The following year he supported Khrushchev's new policy of seeking "peaceful coexistence" with the West, and of opposing Red China's demand for world revolution. "The Chinese," Tito observed, "have overestimated their role in the world."

Despite his enormous popularity at home, he was under constant pressure to permit increasing amounts of Western-style freedom and democracy in his regime. Once he tried to crack down on prospering "little capitalists"—barbers, blacksmiths, bakers, shoemakers, tailors—by raising their taxes seven hundred percent. When ten thousand shops were driven out of business, Yugoslavs found it impossible to get plumbers, electricians, or shoes repaired in less than a month. Indignant grumbling forced Tito to slash the harsh taxes.

His failure to democratize Yugoslavia fast enough disillusioned his old wartime comrade and one-time Vice President, Milovan

Djilas, who criticized him openly in the press. To teach Djilas a lesson, Tito threw him in jail, then let him out with a warning to recant or shut up. Djilas stubbornly persisted in speaking his mind and went back to jail. One of his followers was imprisoned for trying to publish a socialist, but anti-Communist, magazine.

However, Tito was no Stalin. The head of his secret police was another old Partisan comrade, Vice President Aleksandar Ranković, who kept thwarting Communist liberals seeking economic reforms. In 1965, Tito ousted him, apologizing, "Sorry, but the Party, the people, and the country are more important than one individual." He ended the Party's centralized rule by a handful of powerful Communists at the top, and set up a Yugoslav senate of thirty-five leading Party members with real legislative powers. If it was not true democracy in the Western sense, it was at least democracy within the Party.

Another sign of his flexibility was a surprise agreement with the Vatican to establish diplomatic relations, the first of its kind between the Holy See and a Communist nation. Tito agreed to freedom of religion in Yugoslavia, as long as the Church agreed to stay out of politics.

Throughout the 1970s, Tito continued to decentralize the government. The constitution of 1974 turned Yugoslavia into a loose federation of nearly independent republics and provinces with equal status among them. Serbia and Croatia, the two biggest federal units, relinquished considerable influence in the process, and this change led to the rise of a recentralist movement within Serbia that began even before Tito's death.

When Tito died on May 4, 1980, he was hailed as the war hero who saved Yugoslavia; the national hero who welded six divergent Balkan peoples into a unified country; the world hero who defied Josip Stalin and made independence possible for other Communist nations; the respected elder statesman who worked for peaceful coexistence between the Communist and Western worlds.

Yet, the irony of Tito's reign was that he helped sow the seeds for the eventual destruction of his beloved Yugoslavia. He promoted self-governance, yet he never relinquished his party's monopoly of power. He preached peaceful coexistence, but built a powerful army to enforce his rule. He commissioned a federal constitution, but it was one incapable of dealing with disputes among its republics in the absence of his authoritarian oversight.

After Tito's death in 1980, tensions reemerged. Nationalist groups called for more autonomy, which led to declarations of independence in Croatia and Slovenia in 1991. In response, the Serbian controlled Yugoslav army lashed out, resulting in a brutal civil war and the eventual breakup of Yugoslavia.

13

Argentina

Juan Perón (1895–1974)

It was thundering melodrama. Colonel Juan Perón, imprisoned by jealous fellow officers with whom he had seized power in 1943, now lay despairing in a dungeon. His pretty sweetheart Eva Duarte, a blonde radio announcer, swore to save her lover by rallying his followers, the poor workers of Argentina known as *descamisados,* the "shirtless ones."

She called upon them for a giant demonstration of protest on October 17, 1945. Hundreds of thousands of people jammed the streets of Buenos Aires, roaring for the liberation of their champion. The worried military junta in power quickly freed him and promised new elections. Nine days later a jubilant Perón married the girl whose fiery brilliance had saved him.

Shortly afterward Argentina was ruled by something new under the sun in governments—a husband-wife dictatorship.

Born October 8, 1895, in a province of Buenos Aires, Juan Domingo Perón was a typical middle-class Argentine youth— vain, arrogant, convinced that his nation was destined to lead South America as the continent's only civilized country. Sent to military school in 1911, he studied under German instructors, then entered the army. A captain at twenty-nine, he rose rapidly through great personal charm and a masterful air.

In 1930 he was included in a military coup that overthrew a democratically elected, but unpopular, President. The new regime, controlled by the army and wealthy Pampas ranchers, appointed Perón Argentine military attaché to Italy during 1938–39. He was deeply impressed with the aggressive nationalism of Mussolini. Returning home, he studied political theory and pondered whether Il Duce's corporate state could be the wave of the future for Argentina.

During World War II the nation remained neutral. Argentines were restless under the control of the *estancieros,* the old landed aristocracy, and their corrupt rule through a puppet President. In 1943 Perón, now a colonel, felt that the time was ripe to make his personal bid for power. Gathering behind him a group of dissatisfied young army officers from middle-class city families, he engineered a coup.

For three years this military junta ruled the nation as provisional governments rose and fell. Using his powers as Secretary of Labor and Social Welfare, Perón schemed to make himself sole dictator with the support of the *descamisados.* Most Argentine workers now held jobs in city industries rather than on ranches. He let them know he was against the cattle barons, and for giving Argentina a modern economy.

Early in 1944, expressing open admiration for Germany, he began plotting a secret putsch with Argentine Nazis to make himself South America's first Füehrer. He moved toward this goal in 1945 by awarding himself the additional portfolios of Vice President and War Minister. It was at this point that his fellow officers, alarmed by his drive for personal power, decided to arrest and jail him.

When Eva Duarte forced his release, new elections were scheduled for February 1946. A worried United States State Department exposed Perón's plot to create a Nazi Argentina and urged the country to vote against him. Perón accused U.S.

Juan Perón. (*U. S. Information Agency*)

Ambassador Spruille Braden of heading a huge spy ring, and of secretly arming *anti-Perónistas* in Argentina.

Washington's own intervention in Argentine affairs backfired. Always sensitive to interference by the "Colossus of the North," Argentinians went to the polls and elected Perón president by a large majority. Triumphantly promoting himself to general, he quickly amended the constitution to give himself total power. Enthusiastic support for his dictatorship came from the shirtless ones, to whom he promised a steak on every plate—at only six cents a pound.

He broke up the monopolistic holdings of the cattle aristocracy by imposing prohibitive land taxes on huge *estancias.* A sixty per cent raise for city workers lured cowhands away from the pampas into factories. To split up the big ranches even further, Perón passed an edict requiring land inheritances to be divided equally among all heirs.

His new power base among the labor unions made him independent of the military. He was also supported by city industrialists, who, for the first time, had greater influence in Argentina than the *estancieros.* Calling his program for workers *justicialismo*—social justice—he placed it in the hands of his glamorous, shrewd, and energetic wife.

Eva Perón raised wages, shortened working hours, provided holidays with pay, established minimum wages, ensured collective bargaining, set up housing projects for workers, and put social security into effect. She also disbursed gifts and favors to the poor, the widowed, the orphaned, the blind, the sick, the lame. Her clever demagogy and showmanship convinced the *descamisados* that the Peróns really cared about them. They worshiped "Evita" as a goddess.

Meanwhile, Perón worked tirelessly to change Argentina into a modern industrial society. He stimulated the growth of new factories and utilities; took over the British-owned railways; bought out American telephone interests; nationalized the airlines, shipping, and local transportation; financed huge public works. His program was amazingly successful—but at the price of almost bankrupting Argentina.

Billions in national debt began piling up, partly as a result of graft. Perón's personal share of the plunder was estimated at seven hundred million dollars, prudently stashed away in Swiss banks against the day when he might be forced to flee.

The army grumbled at Perón's keeping them on the sidelines while he used trade unions to counterbalance their power. They were outraged when he organized and armed a strong workers' militia, and built a large police force. Perón was using the old dictators' trick of playing off one power group against another. "So long as their surplus energies are used up in fighting one another," he confided to a minister, "they won't have the strength to bother *me* much!"

In true dictator style, also, he silenced opposition by sending hundreds to jail for "political offenses." When he shut down the famous newspaper, *La Prensa,* for criticizing him, other papers quickly took the hint. As one seventeenth-century writer observed, "Tyrants commonly cut off the stairs by which they climb to their thrones."

In 1951, Eva Perón, her appetite for glory sharply whetted, became the *Perónista* Party's candidate for Vice President. This move was too much for the army, which detested her pro-labor activities. Generals mounted a revolt. Perón hastily ordered his wife to withdraw her candidacy, and then purged the army high command. Taking all powers of army promotion and retirement into his own hands, he rewarded those who were loyal, punished those who were not.

He would probably have won the 1951 election even if it had been honest. The Peróns were still popular with the working classes, but not with their bosses. Reckless spending on social welfare had brought the nation's finances dangerously low. His neglect of agriculture had caused a fifty percent drop in wheat and beef exports. The taxpaying middle class, angry at the way he and his henchmen were filling their own pockets, cursed him as a crook, scoundrel, demagogue.

"It does not matter what the rich say about Juan and Evita," one *descamisado* said staunchly, "even if everything they say is true. All we know is that before them we were treated like dirt. It was they who gave us dignity."

In 1952 Eva Perón suddenly died of cancer and was deeply mourned by the working class of Argentina. Many felt that it was she who had been the real brains and heart behind the *Perónista* movement. Deprived of her support, advice, and prestige, Perón began to find himself in trouble.

He turned back to the military for his chief support. At their insistence he offered Washington a Mutual Defense Assistance Pact if the United States would agree to bring the Argentine Army and Navy up to Brazilian strength. Labor unions grew angry at his cultivation of the military. The props of his dictatorship began to melt away.

The industrialists were sick of his graft and financial irresponsibility. The wealthy ranchers hated him. The army still had not forgiven his purge of the high command for opposing Eva. The navy's strong democratic traditions had been hostile to his dictatorship from the outset. Finally, the Catholic Church became outraged when Perón exiled two bishops who dared argue with him. For that offense the Vatican excommunicated him. In intensely Catholic Argentina, that was the last straw. Perón had to go.

In June 1955, the navy and air force joined in a coup to oust him. The plot failed. Perón angrily set street gangs of *descamisados* to fire churches, smash holy statues, and demolish sanctuaries. By September, all three military services united against him. The shirtless ones fought street battles for three days to keep him in power.

But Perón knew that he was finished. He prudently fled to Paraguay, and from there made his way to Spain. He swore to the three million *Perónistas* who remained loyal to him that he would return to Argentina and lead a new revolt.

The military junta in Buenos Aires kept the *Perónistas* off the ballot for seven years, but finally let them run for office in 1962. When they polled about thirty-five percent of the vote, winning forty-five congressional seats, mobs of *descamisados* surged through the streets jubilantly. The worried military declared the election nullified, then dispersed the furious *Perónistas* with tear-gas grenades and fire hoses.

A steady stream of Argentine "tourists" flocked to Madrid to confer secretly with Perón about *"el retorno"* Argentine President Arturo Illia, the new puppet President of the military junta, pretended indifference: "Perón's return is up to Perón." The former dictator swore to return in 1964 and demand new elections. And if the junta refused? "Sometimes in history," he warned grimly, "a civil war has been the only way to save a sinking nation!" The junta took the hint.

When Perón's plane touched down in Rio de Janeiro, it was immediately surrounded by thirty white-helmeted Brazilian police with machine guns. To his dismay he learned that Brazil intended to respect Argentina's plea that he be stopped. Compelled to fly back to Madrid, he faced further humiliation when Franco forced him to sign a pledge giving up all political activity while accepting Spanish asylum.

Perón spent nearly eighteen years in exile, but if Perón himself was defeated, Perónism was not. His name remained a rallying cry in Argentina. He may have been corrupt, a dictator, a demagogue who ruined his country financially. But he was also the leader who broke the power of its landed aristocracy and made it a modern industrial nation. Under Perón, Argentine workers began enjoying the highest standard of living in South America, and achieved a literacy rate of over ninety per cent. Through Perónism, a force greater than the man who gave it his name, Argentina's working class could express discontent against the military and the rich.

Finally in 1973, with the re-establishment of constitutional democracy in Argentina, Perón returned to his country. More than three million Argentinians met him at the airport to welcome him back, and in a special election that fall, he was elected president. But on July 1, 1974, a little over a year after his return, Perón died of a heart attack.

Perón's third wife, Isabel Perón, succeeded him as President, but she was left in a vulnerable position. Unable to establish a base of power, not even among the labor unions who had supported her husband, she was removed from office by a military coup in 1976.

The true revolutionary, most Argentines agree, was Eva Perón. Her memory has become a legend among the shirtless ones, who revere her as a national heroine. They believe that when Perón lost Evita, he lost Argentina.

14

Egypt

Gamal Abdel Nasser (1918–1970)

"Nasser?" said a diplomat stationed in Cairo. "Think of a tiger ready to spring—in any direction. Think of the Sphinx—he's even *more* inscrutable."

Impressive, tall, greying at the temples, with vivid dark eyes, powerful jaw, and confident smile, General Gamal Abdel Nasser was perfectly typecast for the role of Egypt's dynamic strong man which he played for nearly twenty years.

Restlessly chain smoking five packs of American cigarettes during a twelve- to eighteen-hour working day, he insisted upon being phoned at any hour of the night or day when there were important political decisions to make. He trusted only himself.

Born at Beni Mor in upper Egypt on January 15, 1918, he was the son of a humble *fellah* (peasant) who became a post-office employee. As a schoolboy in a land dominated by British colonialism, Gamal regarded George Washington and Gandhi as his personal heroes. Admiration for Voltaire's cynicism, however, led him to view the rise of Hitler and Mussolini as more practical examples to emulate.

While attending school in Alexandria, he joined a local anti-British, pro-Fascist militia called the Greenshirts and became a student leader. He carried their propaganda into the Egyptian Army. In 1942 he was promoted to captain. During four years as

Gamal Abdel Nasser. (*United Nations*)

an instructor in military and staff colleges, he secretly organized a revolutionary clique of young "Free Officers" like Atatürk's Young Turks. They plotted a pan-Arabic federation to free the Middle East of colonialism.

In 1947, the United Nations partitioned Palestine into separate Arab and Jewish states. Egypt and other angry Arab countries launched an attack on the new little nation of Israel. Nasser narrowly escaped death when a bullet hit him a half inch below the heart. The "Free Officers" were embittered by the shoddy equipment supplied them, including shells that wouldn't fire and grenades that exploded in the hand.

Nasser wrote home from the battlefield, "Here we are in the trenches, surrounded by the enemy, engaged in a battle for which we were in no way prepared. The irony of fate! . . . What we are suffering here is only a fraction of what is going on over there in Egypt. Is not our country also being besieged by the enemy, a prey to climbers and traitors?"

When Israel inflicted a humiliating defeat upon the Egyptian Army, Nasser bitterly blamed their corrupt playboy king, Farouk, and his graft-ridden court. The "Free Officers" plotted a revolution. General Mohammed Neguib, an able and honest officer, agreed to give their coup prestige by joining them as a figurehead. On July 22, 1953, their tanks surrounded the fat monarch in his palace at Alexandria.

Farouk was given his choice—abdication and exile, or arrest and imprisonment, "The King of the Casinos" shakily signed his abdication, then left for Capri on the luxury yacht he used to cruise around Europe's gambling resorts.

Neguib assumed the spotlight as leader of the military regime that now ruled Egypt. But true power was in the hands of Lieutenant Colonel Gamal Nasser, who was named Deputy Prime Minister. He was angered when Neguib demanded free elections and began acting like a candidate, seeking support from the fanatical Muslim Brotherhood. Then in October 1954, the

Muslims made an unsuccessful attempt to kill Nasser in Alexandria. Nasser ousted Neguib from office and emerged into the open as Egypt's strong man. Cracking down on the Moslem Party, he had many leaders jailed, beaten, tortured, and hung.

Although he is clearly a dictator, his regime is neither Fascist nor Communist, but something Nasser describes as "Arab Socialism." He confiscated a billion and a half dollars from Egypt's small, wealthy ruling class, but also jailed Communists who opposed him. His aim, he explained, was an honest government that worked for the Egyptian masses, national sovereignty, and a pan-Arabic alliance.

Emerging as the dominant figure of the Middle East, Nasser found himself wooed by both sides of the Cold War. He shrewdly decided to set the United States bidding against Soviet Russia for his favor. Which one, he asked, would help him build the Aswan High Dam, a huge irrigation and power project he needed to turn desert into farmland and provide electricity for new industries? Which one would build up Egypt's military power to let him lead a unified Arab world against Israel?

Secretary of State John Foster Dulles visited Nasser and agreed to help him build Aswan, but offered only limited arms. Moscow, looking for a chance to penetrate the oil-rich Middle East, promptly offered Nasser the arms he wanted without strings. Jubilant, he decided to worry Washington into speeding up action on Aswan. Announcing the arms deal with Russia, he also officially recognized Red China.

It was a tactical blunder. Congress angrily protested against putting up the huge sum necessary to build the Aswan Dam for an Egypt friendly to Communism. Dulles sent Nasser a cold note withdrawing the American offer.

"Choke on your fury!" the Egyptian leader raged at Dulles, whom he castigated as "a rotten old man." Suddenly seizing the Anglo-French Suez Canal Company, he announced that he would finance the Aswan Dam by operating the Canal himself.

The Canal Zone was put under martial law, with every foreign employee warned to stay on the job or go to jail.

The three nations most vitally affected by Nasser's grab of the Canal—Britain, France, and Israel—met in secret to plan a counter-blow. On October 29, 1956, Israeli troops suddenly invaded Egypt. British and French bombers and paratroopers supported the attack. For the second time in a decade, the tough, spirited Israeli Army routed and humiliated the larger but incompetent Egyptian Army.

A dismayed and smarting Nasser could take consolation, however, in world support for Egypt as a victim of aggression. Sir Anthony Eden, Britain's Prime Minister, tried to defend the attack by accusing Nasser of seeking to become "an Egyptian Mussolini" ruling a Middle East empire.

President Eisenhower, embarrassed by his allies' brash act of imperialism, wryly suggested a half-serious solution to his staff: "Tell Nasser we'll be glad to put him on St. Helena and give him a million dollars!" But he felt compelled to publicly disassociate the United States from the Suez invasion, especially with Moscow angrily threatening to launch rocket missiles at London and Paris to compel their retreat.

To Nasser's great relief, United Nations pressure forced an end to the Anglo-French-Israeli invasion, giving him a diplomatic, if not military, triumph. His prestige soared through the Middle East as a hero of Arab nationalism who had boldly robbed the great powers and gotten away with it. Long torn by dynastic feuds because they had lacked a dynamic leader, the Arab nations had apparently found one at last.

The world watched to see what Nasser would do with his prize of Suez. Western cynics predicted that he would let the big ditch fill with silt; that ships sunk by Anglo-French bombs would still block the Canal a decade later; that untrained Egyptians would make an unholy mess of trying to pilot ships through. Nasser determined to show his critics.

Using his best educated technicians, he cleared the Canal and began operating it efficiently. He even widened and deepened it, increasing traffic by ten ships a day. In three years Egypt was earning a hundred sixty million dollars a year from Canal revenues that had once gone to England and France.

Exhilarated, Nasser felt that the Arab world, proud of his accomplishment, was ready to unite behind him, kick out all Western influence in the Middle East, and throw the full might of Moslem hatred against Israel. In February 1958, he took the first step—a merger of Egypt and Syria into the United Arab Republic (UAR), with himself as President.

He now controlled the land through which the great oil pipelines flowed from Iraq to the Mediterranean. The worried monarchs of Jordan, Iraq, and Saudi Arabia, who relied on oil royalties from the West, quickly federated against him. Nasser raged at them as "traitor-kings" to the Arab cause.

The two halves of the divided Muslim world found a dueling ground in Yemen, where a revolutionary group had assassinated the King and precipitated civil war. Nasser sent seventy thousand troops to help the Yemen republicans; Saudi Arabia countered with military aid to the Yemen royalists.

"Brothers!" Nasser appealed to Arab nationalists. "This is not the Yemeni people's battle. It is *our* battle, because the more people we can win over from imperialism and reaction, the more our power is increased. Revolution will soon triumph everywhere." He accused "that pair of nuts"—Jordan's King Hussein and Saudi Arabia's King Saud—of being Western cat's-paws to preserve their thrones and fortunes.

A shrewd propagandist, he used popular Muslim entertainers to sing stirring songs like *We Revolutionists* and *How We Build the High Dam at Aswan* over Radio Cairo's powerful transmitters. When Iraq's throne began tottering, Nasser's voice boomed through their radios: "Arise, my brethren on the police force and the army in Iraq! Stand side by side with your brothers and your people against your enemies!"

Radio Cairo painted glowing pictures of a powerful Arab empire stretching across the Middle East, united under super patriot Gamal Abdel Nasser. But as Arab cynics observed, "The camel driver has his plans, and the camel has his."

In 1961, a coup in Syria overthrew the government, and the new regime pulled out of the United Arab Republic. Alarmed that the revolution might also have roots in Egypt, Nasser made hundreds of arrests, put new editors on all the papers, purged the University of Cairo faculty. He banned all political activity as superfluous. "If I had three political parties," he snapped, "one would be run by the rich, one by the Soviets, and one by the United States!"

Political upheavals in Syria finally brought about a reunion of the United Arab Republic in 1963. Once more hopeful of uniting the Middle East behind his leadership, Nasser called a summit conference of Arab leaders to plan a holy war against Israel.

But three such annual councils failed to produce Moslem unity. "Never in the course of their history," scoffed Tunisia's President Bourguiba, "have the Arabs been more divided, never have they slaughtered each other more ferociously, than since the day Egypt took it upon herself to unite them."

Nasser himself glumly admitted failure: "The object of Arab summits hasn't been achieved. Instead of Arab unity against Palestine, we've had unity of Arab reactionary elements against Arab revolutionary forces." He declined to waste any more time attending the summits "just to say 'how do you do' and drink coffee and tea and go to parties."

He had greater success with his domestic goals. When he first took over Egypt from King Farouk, Arab wits joked that his great ambition was "to raise the peasant to the living standards of the Nile water buffalo." He did considerably better. The *fel-*

lah who once had meat only one day a year now ate it at least once a week. Poor peasants now owned two million acres of land confiscated from big landlords.

Nasser gave his people Egypt's first free medical clinics, and built free primary schools at the rate of four a week. He brought seventy-six thousand women into the nation's economic life as teachers and government workers. And he began to industrialize Egypt, although with great difficulty.

At a Fiat plant near Cairo five thousand workers turned out only fifteen cars a day because of material shortages. Egyptians joked that Nasser didn't have to worry about going to their hell: "There would be no boiling oil (shortage of fuel); the torture rack wouldn't work (no spare parts); the devils wouldn't bother him with pitchforks (true Egyptian civil servants, they signed in at eight and slept the rest of the day)."

Egyptian poverty, a way of life for over two thousand years in that tortured land, still prevailed despite Nasser. Crowded into a narrow strip between deserts, twenty-five million people struggled for bare existence. Even near the end of Nasser's rule, half million were blind; many suffered from malaria; ninety-five per cent were illiterate. Girls married at fifteen, died at forty. Children went hungry. Life was so cheap that professional killers could be hired for a ten-dollar fee.

Each year the high birthrate crowded eight hundred thousand new Egyptians into the country's four per cent of arable land. Nasser's promise of "Plenty for Everyone" was doomed by the population explosion.

Despite a hundred forty million dollars' annual aid in food from the United States, and Soviet aid in building the Aswan Dam, Nasser continued to hold a proudly independent course between them.

In 1965, angered by Washington's secret sale of armaments to Israel through West Germany, Nasser turned mobs loose in an anti-American demonstration. Burning the United States Information Agency library in Cairo, they chanted, "America, withdraw your money for Israel—or Nasser will step on you!" He also ordered one of his MIG's to shoot down a private American plane.

Washington threatened to cut off all aid. "We eat meat four days a week now; we can cut it to three!" Nasser replied defiantly. "We are people of dignity, and do not accept disdain from anyone. Anyone who does not like our attitude can drink the sea!" He charged the United States with demanding that he limit Egyptian armaments under American inspection. "Why not simply announce that our country was an American colony?"

Arresting a United States diplomat as a CIA spy, Nasser accused him of conspiring with the Moslem Brotherhood to fly over the dictator's Alexandria villa and bomb it. A treason trial of fifty-eight "terrorists" in April 1966 resulted in sentences of death and long jail terms for most of them.

Moscow was delighted when Nasser invited Walter Ulbricht, head of Communist East Germany, to visit Egypt and greeted him with a twenty-one-gun salute. Soviet troubleshooter Alexander Shelepin hurried to Cairo to capitalize on Nasser's anger at the United States by tying him to a Moscow-Cairo pact.

The Egyptian dictator coolly refused: "We shall not sell our independence for thirty, forty, or even fifty million pounds."

Cairo wits advised Shelepin: "Try sixty."

In 1967, Nasser grew more receptive to Soviet courting. His failure to unite Middle East rulers behind him, and worsening conditions in Egypt, began to tarnish his reputation as a political leader. Like other dictators who don't know how to cope effectively with domestic problems, he decided to polish his image and divert his people by whipping up a war crisis with Israel. The Soviet Union quickly gave him arms and political support for this adventure, seeing it as a way to swing the Middle East camp into the Russian sphere of influence.

Nasser demanded that the United Nations withdraw its peacekeeping force from Egyptian soil on the Israeli border. He did not really expect the United Nations to comply, but sought to impress other Arab leaders with his boldness. Surprised when Secretary-General U Thant promptly agreed, Nasser felt compelled to make some aggressive moves to show he hadn't been bluffing. He mobilized the Egyptian Army on Israel's borders, and closed the Gulf of Aqaba to Israeli shipping. Israel reacted by rushing its own armed forces into readiness. Nasser then accused Israel of planning aggression against Egypt, and called on the Arab world to unite behind him against Israel. This ruse forced all Arab leaders, including pro-Western King Hussein of Jordan, to pledge to fight under Nasser's leadership or stand condemned as traitors to the Arab cause.

The Israelis, not waiting to be surrounded and crushed by Arab armies, struck swiftly at Nasser's forces in a brilliant, ruthless campaign that destroyed the Egyptian Army and routed Jordanian and Syrian troops. Their victory carried them to the banks of the Suez Canal, to the gates of Damascus, the capital of Syria, and inside Jordan's borders.

The total defeat by Israel in June 1967 discredited and humiliated Nasser. He offered his resignation, but the people of Egypt took to the streets to demonstrate their support, and a vote of confidence by the National Assembly kept him in office.

With his dream of becoming supreme dictator of the United Middle East over, Nasser turned his attention to modernizing his country both militarily and domestically. With support from the Soviet Union, Nasser began upgrading his destroyed military equipment in an attempt to secure his borders with Israel and to reclaim land lost during the June War. The Aswān High Dam was also completed in 1970 after more than ten years of construction. The dam provided increased ability to control floods, provide water for irrigation, and generate electricity, all of which were considered essential to Egypt's continued industrialization.

Although he failed in his quest to unify the Arab world and lost two wars, Nasser was still a popular figure in his country upon his death in 1970, and his passing led to a great outpouring of grief as an estimated 5 million mourners attended his funeral procession.

15

Dictatorship Versus Democracy

If ancient Rome gave the world its first dictatorship, ancient Greece produced the first democracy—a Greek word meaning "rule by the people." The ideas of the early Greeks still characterize the modern democracy. Citizens govern themselves through elected representatives who make the nation's laws. Periodic free elections allow for change, with an honest choice of parties and candidates.

Individuals are secure in their personal liberties and their right to disagree openly with the government. Courts are free to decide all cases on their just merits. The government is committed to the welfare of all its citizens, and not just the benefit of a privileged class. This principle has become highly developed during the twentieth century.

When the new American republic came into existence in 1789, for example, it had serious flaws as a democracy. It permitted slavery, denied the vote to many of the poor, permitted only the educated rich to hold state office. The United States today has greatly broadened its ideas about a democracy's responsibilities to its people. Modern Americans are guaranteed a minimum wage, unemployment benefits, social security, Medicare, universal education, and civil rights.

The idea of democracy has such worldwide popular appeal that even dictators are sometimes forced to pretend that *their* regimes are democracies. Indonesia's Sukarno called his dictatorship a "guided democracy." East Germany's Ulbricht labeled his Communist state the German *Democratic* Republic. Stalin called his rule "democratic centralism."

A dictator's unlimited powers permit him to act more swiftly than a democracy. He can change the course of his government simply by changing his mind. A constitutional democracy, on the other hand, is deliberately slowed down by checks and balances. Power and authority are divided among a President, Congress, and Supreme Court; or a Prime Minister, Parliament, and High Court. These precautions make it difficult for any one man or group to gain enough power to impose a dictatorship.

However, too much division of power can sometimes paralyze a democracy to the extent that it cannot function. For example, the Fourth Republic of France (1946–58) gave perfect representation to all shades of French opinion. But the government was divided into so many splinter parties, which could not agree on a national policy, that one administration after another collapsed until de Gaulle became President.

In a dictatorship there is a strong centralized authority with weak local government. Democracy, on the other hand, depends heavily on self-government at the state, county, city, and town levels. Sharing power often makes the President's job harder, but it is another safeguard against dictatorship.

A Bill of Rights is a key difference between the two forms of government. Americans who take their rights for granted might guard it more zealously if they realized what it is like to live under a dictatorship. An editor who criticizes the government can be thrown in jail and tortured until he confesses to plotting treason. A businessman who refuses to pay graft to a dictator's henchman can have his business confiscated. A student may find his room broken into and searched for forbidden books. A worker who leads a strike can be beaten and imprisoned without trial for years.

To dictators like Hitler and Stalin, individual lives were unimportant. Each killed millions of people without qualm, regarding them as pawns to be sacrificed for the welfare of the state. By contrast, a democracy regards each human life as sacred. Each citizen is protected in his rights under the laws, which stand as a legal shield between him and any official who may seek to persecute him.

In any democracy there are always people or groups that, despite any laws, seek to deprive minorities of their rights. The minorities are not only free to protest, all the way up to the Supreme Court, but they have an *obligation* to protest to keep their democracy strong. "Find out just what people submit to," said abolitionist Frederick Douglass, "and you have found out the exact amount of injustice and wrong which will be imposed upon them . . . till they have resisted."

The nation led by a dictator often gives an impression of greater strength and unity than a democracy, largely because he silences his opposition by a one-party government. His inability to tolerate criticism or admit mistakes is actually a confession of weakness. Italy's one-time dictator felt compelled to bluster, "Mussolini is always right!" Red China was thought to be a monolithic giant until criticism of Mao in 1967 suddenly tore the nation apart, revealing it as a "paper tiger" with serious weaknesses.

A democracy is kept more flexible by the criticism of a free press and of political opponents. When mistakes in government policy are spotlighted, a President or Prime Minister who fails to correct them may be voted out of office. Unlike a dictator, he must be responsive to public opinion.

To allay unrest, the dictator keeps his nation a closed society. He controls press, radio, TV, and movies, using them for propaganda and screening out "subversive" ideas about democracy and freedom. Japan's wartime dictator, Hideki Tojo, forbade the Japanese to harbor any "dangerous thoughts." Hitler Youth were brainwashed by school texts that glorified war, blind obedience to the Fatherland, and Germany's right to rule the world.

Fearful of plots against him, the dictator cannot tolerate free speech. His people are intimidated by secret police who eavesdrop on them and censors who read their mail. Citizens of Stalin's police state who were caught talking to foreigners were arrested as suspected traitors.

A free exchange of ideas, on the other hand, is essential to the democratic way. To rule themselves wisely, the people must be enlightened by open discussion of news and views. They must be free to dissent from, and demonstrate against, government policies they deplore, as many Americans did in protesting the Vietnam War. Significantly, no Russians dared to protest when Khrushchev brutally put down the Hungarian revolt. The only demonstrations permitted in a dictatorship are stage-managed affairs *supporting* a government policy.

Freedom of religion as many Americans know it is rarely tolerated by a dictator. Lenin, an atheist, crushed the power of religion in the Soviet Union. Franco made one church the state religion and persecuted all others.

Life for workers under a dictatorship is sometimes better than it had been for most of them under previous governments. But their unions are either dissolved or controlled by the government. Dictators may also use slave labor, as both Hitler and Stalin did. In a democracy workers are free to bargain for their services through their unions, and can strike if dissatisfied.

The free-enterprise system of democracy has been largely successful in developing a high standard of living for most of its people by encouraging private investment and initiative in developing the nation's economy. The left-wing dictator depends on government control of a planned economy that often suffers from bureaucracy. The right-wing dictator, like Franco, tends to control the economy on behalf of a few powerful industrialists who grow richer through monopoly, while small businesses are crushed and the people live miserably.

Citizens of a democracy honor their President or Prime Minister, but do not turn him into a demigod. The dictator's subjects, in contrast, are brainwashed to believe him a superman above criticism or dismissal. His pictures are carried in parades, plastered on buildings, hung in every home and school. Great rallies are held to glorify him. But his pedestal usually turns out to be much shakier than the democratic platform beneath a President or Prime Minister.

He is forced to suspect in his chief aides the same conspiratorial ambitions that drove him to seize power. Dictators like Chiang Kai-shek and Franco, even though growing old, refuse to designate a successor, fearful that a powerful heir apparent might become impatient and overthrow them.

The government whose stability rests on the life or death of a single man requires its people to live on a powder keg that may blow up at any moment, with complete uncertainty as to what to expect five minutes later. "America is the place," President Woodrow Wilson once said, "where you cannot kill your government by killing the men who conduct it." The tragic assassination of John F. Kennedy in 1963 proved once more the truth of Wilson's observation.

In foreign affairs, the democracy's acceptance of rule by law makes it more likely than a dictatorship to live up to a treaty. Hitler, for example, went back on the Non-Aggression Pact he had signed with Stalin in less than two years. Stalin broke many postwar agreements with the Allies.

The dictator often has a military advantage over the democracy because he depends for his power on a large peacetime army. Normally, popular opinion in a democracy insists upon only a small standing army. The dictator feels freer to strike first, as long as he can be sure of a limited war which will not call into play American atomic missiles.

Because his country usually can't afford both a heavy military program and sufficient consumer goods, the dictator often follows a "guns instead of butter" policy. He needs a big army as much for military control of his people as for foreign adventures. Mao Tse-tung's huge army was intended less for conquest than for suppressing opposition, and for use as an implied threat in international diplomacy.

The dictator's military show of strength is often a cardboard facade that collapses suddenly under pressure. A prime example is Mussolini, whose troops had so little incentive to fight for him that they surrendered by the hundreds of thousands. Citizen-soldiers of a democracy, on the other hand, usually feel that they are fighting in defense of freedoms they believe in and enjoy at home.

The most successful democracies of the world are found in the United States, the British Commonwealth, and Western Europe. Some are ruled by kings and queens who are constitutional monarchs. Often genuinely loved by their people, they are today little more than national symbols, with real power in the hands of an elected parliament.

Not all democracies are perfect, including our own, any more than all dictatorships are wholly evil. Some dictators may, indeed, be building a better life for their people than they have ever known before. As *The Nation* observed, "The cost may be too high in terms of freedom—most Americans would say so—but these people never *had* much freedom."

A dictator may seize power with sincerely patriotic motives, as Mao Tse-tung did when he fought China's feudal lords and corrupt Nationalist troops. But if he stays in power long enough, he often ends up becoming a tyrant. "All power corrupts," said the British historian, Lord Acton, "and absolute power corrupts absolutely."

Could the United States ever become a dictatorship?

Dictators seldom come to power in nations stabilized by a strong, educated, well-to-do middle class; where there are opportunities for the poor to move up the economic ladder through government help, education, training, talent, marriage, or just plain luck. But incredible as it seems, in 1934 one powerful group of right-wing extremists actually mounted a plot to make the United States a dictatorship.

They began spending millions in propaganda to convince Americans that the Roosevelt Administration was Communistic. The next step called for a military hero to lead a private army on Washington "to save America." Taking Roosevelt prisoner, he would broadcast to the nation that he had "overthrown the Communist conspiracy." Congress would be disbanded and the Bill of Rights suspended "for the emergency." Then the plotters would take power through his dictatorship.

Their choice of an American Duce to imitate Mussolini's march on Rome was U.S. Marine General Smedley Butler, twice winner of the Congressional Medal of Honor. The astonished general played along with the conspirators until he had unmasked the whole plot. Then he went to Washington and exposed them before the McCormack-Dickstein Committee of the House of Representatives. His testimony, supported by reliable witnesses, can be found in the *Congressional Record* of December 29, 1934. The plotters quickly disbanded their organization, and the affair was hushed up.

The scheme to make America Fascist, however, was used by Pulitzer Prize novelist Sinclair Lewis as the basis for his 1935 book, *It Can't Happen Here.* Another version of the conspiracy was fictionalized in the book and film, *Seven Days in May.*

To understand how such a thing could happen, it must be remembered that the 1930's were a dangerous period for democracies everywhere. There was terrible unemployment and hunger, and the democracies seemed bewildered by the depression, unable to cope with it. Mussolini, Hitler, and Stalin each urged dictatorship as the only answer.

"One thing is sure . . . democracy is doomed!" the powerful American demagogue, Father Charles Coughlin, cried out in radio broadcasts heard by millions in 1936. "This is our last election. It is Fascism or Communism. We are at the crossroads . . . I take the road of Fascism!"

In 1950 Congress took action to prevent the possibility of a dictatorship of the Left by requiring the American Communist Party to register with the Justice Department as the agent of a foreign power. Party leaders refused to comply and were imprisoned. By 1967, the Party had only some ten thousand members, half of them inactive. Conservatives, however, often charged various protest groups with being Communist-led.

Some prominent American diplomats have warned against demagogues who copy the Fascist technique of using the Red scare to frighten people into supporting oppressive laws; or to give them a scapegoat to blame for political blunders.

"Sinister threats to the rights of individual liberty," Adlai Stevenson warned the United Nations, "are often found concealed under the patriotic cloak of anti-Communism."

Former Ambassador George F. Kennan told the Student Christian Association at Princeton in 1959, "I cannot warn too strongly . . . (against) the suggestion that your personal troubles, or those of the society to which you belong, are attributable only to dimly sensed conspiratorial forces. . . . To accept such suggestions is a sure path to irrationality, to illusion, and to disaster."

In the heated debate that took place in 1966 over American foreign policy, especially in Vietnam, government supporters tended to believe that the interests of democracy required United States support of a right-wing dictatorship against a Communist revolutionary movement. This view has been challenged by John Gunther, the noted journalist, who insisted:

"It is always dangerous for a democracy like the United States to become too closely involved with a dictator or semi-dictator, no matter how convenient this may seem to be. It is the people who count in the long run, and no regime is worth supporting if it keeps citizens down, if only for the simple reason that they will kick it out in time."

As long as Americans can disagree openly with government policy, and as long as we firmly protect each other's personal liberty and freedom as guaranteed in the Bill of Rights, it is unlikely that any dictator, Left or Right, will ever be able to destroy the successful experiment in democracy that began at Philadelphia in 1776.

AFTERWORD

If you thought the days of dictators were done, take a look at Asia, Africa, South America, Cuba, or Eastern Europe. Like an infestation, they're everywhere. They might not walk or talk like Archer's dictators, but that's even scarier. They've learned to evolve with the times. (Although there's always the sadly comic characters, the Kim Jong-uns of the world who close off their countries and rule like it's 1933. Even Russia gave up this brand of a brainwashed, state-run society years ago. Mostly.)

Authoritarian dictators are still very real to us, and half the world is living under their rule. Why does this keep happening?

Archer believed the root of revolution was technology. The world shrank with television and radio, and, according to Archer, poorer countries saw for the first time the way the other half lived. Walking safely to the polls and living past thirty looked pretty nice, so they rose up to take the life they wanted. Ironically, dictators were able to grab power in the chaos— they mobilized through the smooth political stylings of their speeches, and military coups. Today, history continues to repeat itself. The world shrinks, people demand more, and dictators rise to power amid the turmoil.

But there is hope in technology, too. Even on remote mountaintops, crimes against humanity are filmed and broadcast around the world with the swipe of a smartphone. China found that out the hard way when they shot at Tibetan refugees fleeing across the Himalayas in 2006. Video evidence immediately wound up on YouTube. Committing genocide isn't easy anymore. If you aren't safe committing crimes in remote sections of the world, where are you?

Social media may seem like annoying way for our narcissistic friend-of-a-friend to post yet another dinner table selfie or personality quiz result, but it's also the world's most powerful tool for change. It educates us and connects us as never before—it can topple dictators or prop them up, placing the power at our fingertips. Uprisings happen when people are educated, and the internet is quite an education.

Look at the chaotic Arab Spring in 2011. It took one frustrated young man in Tunisia setting himself on fire for the twenty-three-year dictatorship of Ben Ali to crumble into ash. From there, the fire spread across the Arab world in Yemen, Libya, and Egypt. Young people gathered to protest and even oust their dictators. Civil uprisings and demonstrations discharged across a dozen more countries. When the Syrian regime of Bashar al-Assad blocked reporters from exposing their violent, sniper-gun-suppression, intrepid bloggers still found a way to post the videos. And that's not all social media is good for.

Thanks to Twitter, angry citizens posted where they would be and when, allowing them to achieve critical mass. Tweets increased from 2,300 tweets a day to 230,000 the week leading up to Egyptian president Hosni Mubarak's resignation, and when the government tried to shut down social media, people went to the streets to dissent. But just as Archer laid out, another dictator through a military coup has already taken root in the chaos. History repeats.

Egypt now lives with "President" Sisi, and Syria, Yemen, and Libya have collapsed into civil war. Will we never be free?

That takes us back to Archer's point. Why did he write a book about dictators in the first place? It wasn't to glorify them or to teach us how to bully others around. His point was to help us better understand dictators and the conditions under which they rise to power so that we can "keep the democratic world secure in its freedoms".

This means looking at the ways dictators have changed. With technology, everything is subtler. Dictators don't rule with "perfect" approval ratings anymore—they let some opponents win on enough ballots to keep suspicion low. They have constitutions, elections, and the internet. The difference lies in the details.

We can't take our freedoms for granted. As Archer points out, the Bill of Rights is a key difference between dictatorship and democracy. It's what gives us freedom to criticize our government and express our opinions without spending the next twenty years doing hard labor.

Another difference is the sharing of power. A truly democratic president has a series of checks and balances to keep their fist from becoming too iron. It doesn't make the job easy, and a leader definitely shouldn't have time to stockpile cash in an offshore bank account. Their reelection depends on listening to their voters and making changes.

While these components may not be perfect in practice, they are better than living under the arbitrary whims of an absolute dictator or even an "enlightened" one. We must protect our liberty and our democracy. Freedom needs to be fought for continuously, and if the Arab Spring has taught us anything, it's that we must keep fighting. Otherwise, the dictators have won.

BIBLIOGRAPHY

Adams, Sherman. *Firsthand Report.* New York: Harper & Brothers, 1961.

Archer, Jules. *Battlefield President: Dwight D. Eisenhower.* New York: Julian Messner, 1967.

———. *Laws That Changed America.* New York: Criterion Books, Inc., 1967.

———. *Man of Steel: Josip Stalin.* New York: Julian Messner, 1965.

———. *Twentieth Century Caesar: Benito Mussolini.* New York: Julian Messner, 1967.

Ayling, S. E. *Portraits of Power.* New York: Barnes & Noble, Inc., 1963.

Blanshard, Paul. *Democracy and Empire in the Caribbean.* New York: The Macmillan Company, 1947.

Coles, S. F. A. *Franco of Spain.* London: Neville Spearman, 1955.

Collier, Basil. *Barren Victories: Versailles to Suez.* Garden City, New York: Doubleday & Company, Inc., 1964.

Crankshaw, Edward. *Gestapo, Instrument of Tyranny.* New York: The Viking Press, Inc., 1956.

De Launay, Jacques. *Secret Diplomacy of World War II.* New York: Simmons-Boardman, 1963.

Djilas, Milovan. *Conversations with Stalin.* New York: Harcourt, Brace & World, Inc., 1962.

Dubois, Jules. *Fidel Castro.* Indianapolis, New York: The Bobbs-Merrill Company, Inc., 1959.

Fischer, Louis. *The Life of Lenin.* New York: Harper & Row, Publishers, 1964.

FitzGibbon, Constantine. *Officers' Plot to Kill Hitler.* New York: Avon Books, 1956.

Forman, Harrison. *Report from Red China.* New York: Henry Holt and Company, 1945.

Fremantle, Anne, ed. *Mao Tse-tung.* New York: New American Library, 1962.

Galvao, Henrique. *Santa Maria: My Crusade for Portugal.* Cleveland and New York: The World Publishing Company, 1961.

Gamier, Christine. *Salazar.* New York: Farrar, Straus & Young, 1954.

Goerlitz, Walter. *History of the German General Staff.* New York: Frederick A. Praeger, 1959.

Griffith, Ernest S., ed. *Fascism in Action.* Washington: U.S. Government Printing Office, 1947.

Gunther, John. *Inside Europe Today.* New York: Harper & Brothers, 1961.

————. *Inside Asia.* New York and London: Harper & Brothers, 1939.

————. *Inside Latin America.* New York and London: Harper &Brothers, 1941.

————. *Inside Russia Today.* New York: Harper & Brothers, 1957.

Hassett, William D. *Off the Record with F.D.R.* London: George Allen & Unwin Ltd., 1960.

Hertland, W. E. *A Short History of the Roman Republic.* Cambridge, England: Cambridge University Press, 1929.

Hicks, Albert C. *Blood in the Streets.* New York: Creative Age Press, Inc., 1946.

Hitler, Adolf. *My Battle.* Boston and New York: Houghton Mifflin Company, 1933.

Household, H. W. *Rome: Republic and Empire.* London: J. M. Dent and Sons, Ltd., 1936.

Hughes, Emmet John. *The Ordeal of Power.* New York: Atheneum, 1963.

Kalckreuth, Dunbar von. *Three Thousand Years of Rome.* New York, London: Alfred A. Knopf, 1930.

Kennan, George F. *Russia and the West Under Lenin and Stalin.* Boston: Little, Brown and Company, 1960.

King-Hall, Stephen. *Our Times.* New York: Horizon Press, 1962.

Lieu wen, Edwin. *Arms and Politics in Latin America.* London, New York: Frederick A. Praeger, 1961.

Ludwig, Emil. *Talks with Mussolini.* Boston: Little, Brown and Company, 1933.

Monelli, Paolo. *Mussolini,* New York: The Vanguard Press, Inc., 1954.

Nehemkis, Peter. *Latin America: Myth and Reality.* New York and Toronto: The New American Library, 1964.

Parkes, Henry Bamford. *A History of Mexico.* Boston: Houghton Mifflin Company, 1960.

Payne, Robert, ed. *The Civil War in Spain.* Greenwich, Conn.: Fawcett Publications, Inc., 1962.

Radler, D. H. *El Gringo.* Philadelphia and New York: Chilton Company, 1962.

Seldes, George. *One Thousand Americans.* New York: Boni & Gaer, 1947.

Shirer, William L. *The Rise and Fall of the Third Reich.* New York: Simon and Schuster, 1962.

Stilwell, Josip W. *The Stilwell Papers.* New York: Macfadden-Bartell Corporation, 1962.

Suetonius. *The Twelve Caesars.* Baltimore: Penguin Books, 1957.

Tannenbaum, Frank. *Ten Keys to Latin America.* New York: Alfred A. Knopf, 1962.

Trevor-Roper, H. R. *The Last Days of Hitler.* New York: The Macmillan Company, 1947.

Truman, Harry S. *1945: Year of Decisions.* Garden City, New York: Doubleday & Company, Inc., 1955.

———. *1946–1952: Years of Trials and Hope.* Garden City, New York: Doubleday & Company, Inc., 1956.

Wells, H. G. *The Outline of History.* New York: Doubleday & Company, Inc., 1949.

Werth, Alexander. *Russia at War.* New York: E. P. Dutton, 1964.

Wint, Guy. *Spotlight on Asia*. London: Penguin Books, 1959.

Wise, David, and Thomas B. Ross. *The Invisible Government*. New York: Random House, Inc., 1964.

Wolfe, Bertram D. *Three Who Made a Revolution*. New York: The Dial Press, 1961.

Magazines: many issues were consulted of *Newsweek, The Nation, Time, Life,* and *The Saturday Evening Post. Special reports:* Center for the Study of Democratic Institutions, Santa Barbara, California. *Official government publications:* these were supplied to me by the governments of the Soviet Union, the Republic of China (Formosa), Indonesia, and Yugoslavia.

Index

Acton, John Emerich, 178
Aidit, 137, 140, 141, 142
Alexander I, King, 149
Alexander III, Tsar, 14
Alfonso XIII, King, 126, 133
Alliluyeva, Nadya, 25–26
death of, 27
Anglo-French Suez Canal Company, 165
Argentina, 5, 154–161
election of 1962, 160
Nazi Party in, 155
Aswan High Dam, construction of, 165, 169
Avanti, 39
Azaña, Manuel, 126

Badoglio, Pietro, 44, 45
Bakunin, Mikhail, 37
Balart, Mirtha Díaz, 87
Bandung Institute of Technology, 135
Bao Dai, 9
Barnes, Father, 77
Barrera, Antonio Imbert, 80
Baruch, Bernard, 19

Batista, Fulgencio, 81–86, 87, 88, 89, 90, 91
background of, 81–82
executions of, 85
exiled, 86, 90
gangster dealings, 84, 85
Bay of Pigs invasion, 93–94
Beer Hall Putsch, the, 118
Berlin airlift, the, 29
Betancourt, Rómulo, 80
Blackshirts (private army), 7, 117
beginning of, 41
Blue Division (World War II), 129
Blue Shirts (secret police), 59, 62
Bourguiba, Habib, 168
Boxer Rebellion, 55
Braden, Spruille, 157
Braun, Eva, 123
Brest Litovsk, Treaty of, 18
Brezhnev, Leonid, 5, 37
Brownshirts (private army), 119
Brussels Congress (1903), 16
Buddhism, 64
Bulganin, Nikolai, 32, 33
Bulge, Battle of the, 123

Butler, Smedley, 179

Caesar, Julius, 3, 43
Cairo Conference, 61
Caliphate, the, 48, 52
Cárdenas, Lazaro, 6
Castro, Fidel, 6, 7, 36, 84, 85,
    86–98
background of, 86–87
executions of, 91
in exile, 89
as a lawyer, 84, 87
reform programs, 92
U.S. visit, 92
Castro, Juanita, 86, 95
Castro, Ramón, 92
Castro, Raúl, 86, 89, 92
Central Intelligence Agency
    (CIA), 93, 138, 170
Chamberlain, Neville, 120
Chang Hsueh-liang, 59
Charles I, King, 3
Chetniks (army), 146
Chetwode, Philips, 129
Chiang Kai-shek, 5, 56–63, 64,
    66, 67, 68, 69, 177
background of, 56
birth of, 56
exiled, 69
massacres communists, 57, 64
Chiang Kai-shek, Madame, 59,
    60
Chibás, Eduardo, 87
China, 8, 37, 55–71, 112, 137,
    151, 165, 175, 178, 182
cultural purges, 70

denounces Khrushchev, 37
Five-Year Plan, 69
missile programs, 70
Napoleon I on, 55
rift with U.S.S.R., 70
World War II, 60, 68
Chou En-lai, 59, 139
Chu Teh, 63
Churchill, Randolph, 149
Churchill, Sir Winston, 18, 121,
    130, 146, 149
Coimbra University, 5, 108, 109
Cold War, 150, 165
beginning of, 29
Columbia Broadcasting System
    (CBS), 79
Communism, 8, 20, 27, 28, 34,
    94, 95, 113, 138, 139, 165, 180
beginning of, 14
Lenin on, 20
party congresses, 16, 21, 27, 33
Communist Manifesto (Marx and
    Engels), 11
Communist Party (Cuba), 83, 90
Communist Party (U.S.S.R.)
beginning of, 16–17
birthday calendar of, 37
early factions of, 16–17
1903 Brussels Congress, 16
Twentieth Congress, 33
Communist Party (United
    States), 180
Costa, Manuel da, 109
Coughlin, Father Charles, 180
Craig, Malin, 82
Cromwell, Oliver, 3, 6

Cruz, Felipe de la, 96
Cuba, 5, 7, 8, 36, 81–104
Bay of Pigs invasion, 93–94
Communist Party, 83, 90
1933 revolution in, 76
per capita income (1967), 96
Cuban missile crisis (1962), 36, 94

Darwin, Charles, 82
Davis, Joseph E., 27
De Gaulle, Charles, 123, 174
"Death to Intelligence!" (slogan), 127
Delgado, Humberto, 111
Democracies
compared to dictatorships, 173–181
U.S. foreign policy and, 180
number of, 2
popular appeal of, 174
world's first, 173
Depression of 1929, 126
in Germany, 118
Dessalines, Jean Jacques, 101, 104
Diaz, Porfirio, 4, 7
Dictators
definition of, 1
prototype of, xv–xxii
types of, 3–4
Dictatorships
Bakunin on, 37
compared to democracy, 173–181
U.S. foreign policy and, 180

left wing, 8, 176
first, 3
meaning of, 2
nature of, 1–10
number of, 2
plot for U.S., 179
right-wing, 8, 72, 177
meaning of, 2
world's first, 173
Djilas, Milovan, 144, 152
Djugashvili, Joseph Vissariono-vich, see Stalin, Joseph
Dolfuss, Engelbert, 120
Dominican Republic, 8, 72, 73–80, 86
Dorticós, Osvaldo, 94
Douglass, Frederick, 175
Dulles, John Foster, 85, 138, 165
Duvalier, François, 4, 5, 98–104
model city program of, 100, 101
private militia of, 7
terror reign of, 102–103

Eastman, Max, 9
Eden, Anthony, 166
Egypt, 7, 8, 162–172
Anglo-French-Israeli invasion of, 166
first free medical clinics in, 169
population, 169–170
Eisenhower, Dwight D., 28, 34–36, 72, 80, 85, 92, 93, 122, 123, 130, 137, 147, 151, 166
snubs Castro, 92
on U-2 spy plane incident, 35–36

Engels, Friedrich, 11
Enver Pasha, 50
Ethiopia, invasion of (1935), 43

Farouk, King, 164, 168
Fascism, 6, 42–46, 101, 103, 127
Hitler on, 9
in Italy, 27, 41–46
election of 1921, 41
opposition to, 41
in U.S., 179–180
Five-Year Plans
China, 69
U.S.S.R, 26
Forli Socialist Federation, 39
Fourteen Points (Wilson), 18
Franco, Francisco, 4, 6, 27, 110,
    113, 124–133, 160, 176, 177
background of, 124
birth of, 124
meets Hitler, 129
opposition to, 130–133
proclaimed caudillo, 129
slogan of, 127
Free Officers (organization), 164
Freeman, Orville L., 36
French Revolution, 3, 4

Galindez, Jesus Maria de, 79
Galvão, Henrique, 112
Gardner, Arthur, 85
Germany, 4, 18, 27, 28, 29, 34,
    43, 50, 78, 114–123
Depression of 1929, 118
mark inflation (1923), 108
Non-Aggression Pact, 120, 177

Reichstag fire of 1933, 119
Weimar Republic, 115, 118
World War 1, 115
World War II, 121–123
Goebbels, Joseph, 118, 119, 122
Goering, Hermann, 117, 121
Gorky, Maxim, 19
Great Britain
acquires Hong Kong, 55
Labour Party in, 29
Great Leap Forward (program),
    69
Green Shirts (militia), 162
Guernica, bombing of (1937),
    128
Guernica (painting), 128
Guevara, Che, 89
Gunther, John, 53, 131, 180

Haile Selassie, Emperor, 104
Haiti, 4, 5, 77, 98–104
per capita income, 100
population, 100
Trujillo's massacres (1937),
    76–77
U.S. invasion of (1914), 101
Haider, Franz, 123
Halide Edib, 48, 53
Hammarskjöld, Dag, 36
Hassett, William, 61
Hemingway, Ernest, 127
Hindenburg, Paul von, 118, 119
Hitler, Adolf, 5–7, 27, 28, 43–45,
    111, 114–123, 127, 128, 129,
    135, 146, 147, 149, 162, 175,
    176, 177, 180

attempted assassination of, 114, 122

background of, 115

beer hall putsch, 118

birth of, 115

death of, 123

on fascism, 9

on Jews, 119, 121

meets Franco, 129

Mussolini and, 44, 45, 117

Spanish Civil War and, 44, 120, 128

Hitler Youth Organization, 176

Ho Tzu-ch'un, 64

Hong Kong, British acquisition of, 55

Hugenberg, Alfred, 118

Hugo, Victor, 84

Hungary, anti-communist uprising in, 33, 150

Hussein, King, 167, 171

Illia, Arturo, 160

Indonesia, 5, 134–143

Dutch rule of, 134–135

massacre of communists in, 142

per capita income, 137

Indonesian Nationalist Party (PNI), 135

Inquisition, the, 126

International Brigade (Spanish Civil War), 127

Iskra (magazine), 15, 23

Israel

established, 164

invades Egypt (1956), 166–167

invades Egypt (1967), 171

It Cant Happen Here (Lewis), 179

Italy, 4–6, 27, 38–46

Fascist Party in, 27, 41–46

election of 1921, 41

opposition to, 41

invades Ethiopia, 43

Socialist Party in, 39

Jews, 78, 115, 117

Hitler on, 119, 121

Italy's persecution of, 44

in World War II death camps, 121

Johnson, Hugh, 77

Johnson, Lyndon B., 35, 72, 95

Kamenev, Lev Borisovich, 25, 26, 27

Kaplan, Fanny, 19

Kazan University, 14

Kemal Atatiirk, 7, 47–54

background of, 47–48

birth of, 47

death of, 54

modernization reforms of, 52

opposition to, 53

Kennan, George F., 8, 21, 23, 24, 180

Kennedy, John F., 36, 72, 92–94, 103, 139

assassination of, 95, 177

Cuban missile crisis, 95

Kerensky, Alexander, 12, 16, 17, 149

Khrushchev, Nikita, 5, 29–37, 150, 151, 176
background of, 29–30
birth of, 29, 37
Cuban missile crisis and, 36
denounces Stalinism, 32, 69
ousted from leadership, 37
U.S. tour, 35–37
Korean War, 29, 69
Kosygin, Aleksey, 5, 37
Krupskaya, Nadya, 15
Kun, Béla, 20–21
Kuomintang, 55–57, 60–62, 66, 68
alliances with communists, 57
brutality of, 61
desertions from, 60
Ky, Nguyen Cao, 9

Labour Party (Great Britain), 29
League of Nations, 43, 120
Lenin, Vladimir Ilyich, 5, 8, 9, 12–21, 24, 25
attempted assassination of, 19
background of, 14–15
birth of, 12–14
on communism, 20
death of, 21
Lewis, Sinclair, 179
Life, 79
Lin Piao, 66
Lippmann, Walter, 9
Livy, Titus Livius, 2
Llorente, Armando, 90
Lloyd George, David, 12

McCormack-Dickstein Committee, 179
Machado, Gerardo, 76, 81
Madero, Francisco, 4
Madrid University, 130, 132
Magloire, Paul, 102
Malenkov, Georgi, 32
Malraux, André, 127
Manchu dynasty, 55, 64
Manchuria, Japanese invasion of (1931), 59
Manuel II, King, 108
Mao Tse-tung, 9, 37, 56, 57, 63–71, 178
background of, 64
birth of, 64
March, Juan, 127
Marshall, George, 61
Marx, Karl, 8, 9, 11, 14, 35, 82, 135
Matthews, Herbert, 90
Mein Kampf (Hitler), 9, 115, 117, 119, 121
Mensheviks (Communist Party), 16–17
Mexico, 4, 7, 77, 89, 95
Spanish Civil War and, 128
Trotsky in, 26
Mihailovich, Draza, 146, 149
Mikoyan, Anastas, 33
Milan Fighters Fascio (organization), 41
Mitka, 24
Monarchy
absolute, 1
constitutional, 133, 178

Spanish fascism and, 127
Morrison, Herbert, 29
Moslem Brotherhood, 165,
    167–168, 170
Mussolini, Benito, 5, 6, 7, 38–46,
    117, 118, 120, 123, 127, 129,
    178–180
background of, 38–39
birth of, 38
executed, 46
Hitler and, 44, 45, 117
marches on Rome, 41
Spanish Civil War and, 44, 127

Napoleon I, 4, 55, 64, 101
on China, 55
Nasser, Gamel Abdel, 7, 8,
    162–172
accomplishments of, 169
background of, 162–163
birth of, 162
seizes Suez Canal, 165
Nasution, 141, 142
Nation, The, 93
National Liberation Army
    (Yugoslavia), 149
Nazi Party, 27, 28, 117, 118
in Argentina, 155
industrialists' support of, 118
Storm Troopers, 7
Neguib, Mohammed, 164, 165
New York Times, The, 78, 90
Nicholas I, 11
Nixon, Richard M., 92
Nkrumah, Kwame, 9

Non-Aggression Pact
    (Germany-U.S.S.R.), 120, 177
North Atlantic Treaty Organiza-
    tion (NATO), 29, 111
Nuclear test ban treaty (1963),
    70

OGPU (secret police), 7
Okhrana (secret police), 21
Onaindia, Alberto de, 128
Open Door Policy, 55
Operation Barbarossa (World
    War II), 121–122
Opium War, 55
Organization of American
    States (OAS), 80
Ottoman Empire, 47–48

Papen, Franz von, 118
Patman, Wright, 127
Peace Corps, 141
Peking University, 64
Perón, Eva, 154–159, 161
death of, 159
Perón, Juan Domingo, 5,
    154–161
background of, 154–155
birth of, 154
excommunicated, 159
exiled, 159–161
reform programs, 157
Petrovna, Nina, 30
Picasso, Pablo, 128
PKI (Marxist organization), 137,
    141
Pla y Deniel, Cardinal, 131

Plato, 82, 86, 140
Pope, Allen, 138
Popolo d'Italia, 39, 41
Portugal, 5, 8, 105–113
declared Republic (1910), 108
1933 Constitution, 106, 109
overseas colonies of, 112–113
Portuguese Legion (Spanish
  Civil War), 110
Potsdam Conference, 130
Pravda, 32
Prensa, La, 158
Princeton University, 180
Prío, Carlos, 84, 87

Radio Cairo, 167
Ranković, Aleksander, 152
Rasputin, Grigori Efimovich, 11
Red Army (China), 59–62
defeats Chiang Kai-shek, 61
Long March of, 63–71
beginning of, 63–64
end of, 71
miles covered, 64
Red Guards (China), 55, 70
Reichstag fire of 1933, 119
Reign of Terror (French
  Revolution), 3
Republic, The (Plato), 86
Republican Loyalists (Spanish
  Civil War), 127–129
Revolution of 1905 (U.S.S.R.),
  11, 24
Revolution of 1917, 17, 24, 30
beginning of, 16
Rivera, Primo de, 126

Robespierre, Maximilien, 3
Roehm, Ernst, 117, 119
Roman Empire, 2–3
Rome-Berlin-Tokyo Axis, 120
Rommel, Erwin, 122
Roosevelt, Franklin D., 60, 72,
  78, 101
Roosevelt, Mrs. Franklin D., 61
Rosenberg, Alfred, 117
Rousseau, Jean-Jacques, 3
Royal Air Force (RAF), 121
Rundstedt, Karl Rudolf Gerd
  von, 123
Russian Orthodox Church, 28

St. Louis Post-Dispatch, 93
Salazar, Antonio de Oliveira, 5,
  8, 105–113
background of, 106–108
birth of, 106
Spanish Civil War and, 110
university lecturing of, 108–109
Santa Maria (liner), 112
Saragossa Academy, 126
Saud, King, 167
Second Socialist International,
  16
Seven Days in May (motion
  picture), 179
Shelepin, Alexander, 170
Smith, Earl, 85
Social Democratic Labor Party,
  15, 23
Social Revolutionaries
  (organization), 19

Socialism, 12, 16, 18, 24, 93, 122, 135, 149
Spain, 4, 27, 44, 124–133
Spanish Civil War, 44, 110, 126–128
    beginning of, 126–127
    bombing of Guernica, 128
    fall of Madrid (1939), 128
    Hitler and, 44, 120, 128
Spanish Foreign Legion, 126
Spengler, Oswald, 82
Sputnik (satellite), 33
Stalin, Joseph, 5, 7, 17, 21–29, 56, 69, 120–121, 146, 147, 149, 152, 174, 176, 177
    background of, 21, 23–24
    birth of, 23
    death of, 29, 32, 69
    marriages of, 24
    purges of, 27
    rift with Tito, 150
    in Tiflis Seminary, 23
    Trotsky feuds, 24, 25
    as Tsar's agent, 30
    Twentieth Party Congress on, 33
Stauffenberg, Claus von, 114
Stevenson, Adlai, 180
Stilwell, Joseph, 56, 60
    death of, 61
Student Christian Association, 180
Subandrio, 139, 140, 141
Suez Canal, seizure of, 165–166
Suharto, General, 141, 142
Sukarno, Achmed, 5, 7, 134–143

    arrested, 142
    background of, 134–135
    birth of, 134
    exiled, 143
Sulla, Lucius Cornelius, 3
Sun Yat-sen, 55–56
Suslov, Mikhail, 35, 37
Svanidze, Katherine, 24

Thant, U, 171
Third International Congress, 20
Thomaz, Americo, 111
Tiflis Theological Seminary, 23
Time, 79
Tito, Joseph Broz, 5, 8, 33, 144–153
    background of, 148–149
    birth of, 148
    rift with Stalin, 150–151
Tocqueville, Alexis de, 2
Tojo, Hideki, 176
Toledo Academy, 124
Tonton Macoutes (militia), 7, 102–104
Toussaint L'Ouverture, Pierre Dominique, 101
Trotsky, Leon, 18, 20, 24–26
    assassinated, 26
    feuds with Stalin, 24, 25
Trujillo Molina, Rafael Leonidas, 8, 73–80, 87
    assassinated, 80
    background of, 73
    massacres Haitian Negroes (1937), 76–77

Trujillo Molina, Ramfis, 75, 79
Truman, Harry, 28, 29, 62, 92
Truman Doctrine, 29
Tshombe, Moise, 9
Turkey, 7, 36, 47–54
    neutrality of, 54
    World War I, 48–50
Twentieth Congress
    (Communist Party), 33

U-2 spy plane incident, 35
Ulbricht, Walter, 170
Union of Soviet Socialist
    Republics, 5, 11–37
New Economic Policy, 19
Non-Aggression Pact (1939),
    120, 177
Revolution of 1905, 11, 24
Revolution of 1917, 16–17, 24, 30
beginning of, 12
rift with China, 69–70
Spanish Civil War and, 128
World War I, 11–12, 16–17
World War II, 5, 28–29, 32, 121
casualties, 27–28
See also Communist Party
    (U.S.S.R.)
United Fruit Company, 81, 87
United Nations, 93, 112, 130,
    137, 149, 151, 166, 170
Food and Agriculture
    Organization, 140
Khrushchev's shoe banging at,
    36, 37
partitions Palestine, 164
Trusteeship Council, 112

United States
communism in, 180
dictatorship plot, 179
fascism in, 179–180
foreign policy, 180–181
invasion of Haiti (1914), 101
United States Constitution, 174,
    181
United States Information
    Agency (Cairo), burning of,
    169–170
University of Cairo, 168
University of Havana Law
    School, 86–87

Vásquez, General Horacio, 73
Vatican, 152
excommunicates Peron, 159
Versailles Treaty, 51, 115, 117,
    120, 148
Victor Emmanuel, King, 41, 44
Vincent, President, 77
Voodoo, 100

Washington, George, 64
Weimar Republic, 115, 118
Werth, Alexander, 131
White Paper on China (U.S.), 61
White Russian Army, 18, 20–21,
    25, 148
Wilson, Woodrow, 17–18, 177
World War I, 11–12, 16–18, 39,
    50, 115, 148
World War II, 5, 28–29, 32,
    60–62, 68–69, 121–123, 129,
    144–149

Battle of the Bulge, 123
beginning of, 28
end of, 28–29
extermination camps, 121
neutrality, 54, 111, 155
Operation Barbarossa, 121–122
scorched earth policy, 28

Yemen war, 167
Yezhov, Nikolay Ivanovich, 27
Young Turks (society), 48
Yugoslavia, 8, 33, 144–153

Zinoviev, Nikolay
    Nicolayevich, 27